MOCKTAILS

MORE THAN 50 RECIPES FOR DELICIOUS NON-ALCOHOLIC COCKTAILS, PUNCHES, AND MORE

Text and recipes by Richard Man
Photography by Simon Bajada
Translated by Gun Penhoat

Racehorse Publishing

CONTENTS

FOREWORD

I have worked with alcoholic beverages since I was fifteen years old—OK, eighteen then, so as not to ruffle any feathers. I grew up in a popular tavern environment that has a long-standing place in Swedish food culture and is near and dear to the heart of the Swedish everyman. A typical meal is comprised of four small entrées with a sweet and sour sauce and ending with a dessert of deep-fried banana à la mode . . . you know the drill. My parents arrived in Sweden from Hong Kong to try their luck during the 1960s and '70s. Their recipe for success turned out to be a Chinese hole-in-the-wall restaurant and a bar with musical entertainment in an industrial town in the province of Dalarna/Dalecarlia. In that bar, I got to know all the syrupy '90s crooners and learned to mix a grog. The latter took me to bartending jobs in Stockholm, London, New York, Barcelona . . . the world. During this journey the grog progressively morphed into cocktails, while I transformed myself from a hip guy from Dalecarlia into a nerd—a food and beverage nerd. I am such a geek that I also got myself a masters' degree in Chemical Engineering from KTH (Kungliga Tekniska Högskolan—The Royal Institute of Technology), not because I wanted to dabble in nanotechnology, but because food and drink, in its purest form, is just that—chemistry. Through the years I've held titles such as tavern keeper, sommelier, and Bacardi Ambassador, and was named Innovator of The Year by the Swedish Bartenders' Association in 2016.

I love my job, but alcohol in and of itself has never been the main attraction for me; it's the experience I can create and deliver to a guest that inspires me. This is the skill I have always wanted to develop. Many of my own favorite food and beverage experiences have been alcohol-free. It's probably because they took place in cultures where alcohol doesn't feature as prominently as it does in Swedish life. However, in Sweden, celebrations, holidays, and other festive occasions are typically associated with the consumption of alcohol, whether we're hosting a dinner at home or we're invited to a party.

My first real eye-opener with non-alcoholic beverages in combination with food happened when my wife and I were expecting our first child. We often ate in restaurants, and the restaurants we frequented had ambitions to provide great food, drink, and service. Sadly, it quickly became obvious how the experience can be ruined when neither high-standard service nor well-thought-out drink recommendations take the teetotal dining guest into consideration. Hoping to improve the situation, I started to look for tannins in tomato stalks and pleasing sipping quality through means other than alcohol strength. At the same time, I got involved in the Fotografiska's (The Museum of Photography) venture focusing on alcohol-free bar offerings and mindful consumption, and the food and beverage nerd in me reemerged.

Over the last few years I have also put a lot of effort into pairing alcohol-free beverages with food. I have done this so often that I now feel that I have something to contribute on the subject—something to add to the discussion. A drink must taste good, whether it contains alcohol or not. A beverage served with food must suit the food, whether the beverage is alcoholic or not. And your dinner company must enjoy a fantastic experience, with or without drinking alcohol.

PAIRING FOOD & DRINK

If you know which dish you want to prepare, look at the list below to find a suitable drink to serve with it. For a more complete explanation of each food category, check out pages 20 to 22.

PAIRING FOOD & DRINK

A successful food and drink combo can happen anywhere. Maybe the supermarket's new breakfast juice makes the chia pudding actually taste edible. The new coffee machine at work can turn the afternoon break into something more than a mere lifesaving pause. Or perhaps the invitation to the Nobel Dinner arrives and you will be able to experience the culmination of hours of painstaking combination planning. Anyone can tell when something doesn't work. You don't need to be an educated sommelier to understand that toothpaste and orange juice is a bad mix. But if you take an interest in food and drink, you'll immediately notice when you stumble on that great combination at the breakfast table or at the coffee machine. Perhaps you would also like to know why this particular combination is such a success? There are quite a few tips and tricks for you to find along the road. Call them what you will: philosophies, theories, rules, or whatever. Read them. Learn from them. But never take them so seriously that they remove the fun from it all.

THE ROLE OF THE MEALTIME BEVERAGE

A mealtime drink can serve many functions. Perhaps you drink because you're thirsty, perhaps because you're in the mood for a certain drink, or perhaps because you need it to help you swallow your food. You might also feel that you want something more from your drink. Naturally, you'll want something nice to drink when you have prepared a really nice meal. The beverage should taste great on its own, but also suit the food you've taken care to prepare. This book is about the latter kind of drink—the drink that both tastes good and goes with the food you eat.

A successful food and drink combination can heighten either the food experience or the drink experience. In the best-case scenario, the food and the drink will boost each other's qualities and contribute to the whole package, including the ambience, resulting in a greater social atmosphere. Your drink has just the right amount of acidity and freshness, the food on the plate is in perfect harmony, the summer evening feels a few degrees warmer, and suddenly your date is more attractive. If you've ever had this experience, you probably thought that it was due to the alcohol in the drink. It did its job and made everything seem just a little better. You might be right in your assumption. However, I'm now going to show you that the same effect can be had without alcohol adding in its two cents.

We have a few more things to cover while we're on the subject of atmosphere and social mood. The role of some mealtime drinks is purely social. Imagine that you're giving a dinner party at home. You go to a high-end wineshop and tell the person behind the counter what type of meal you're going to serve, and that you're wondering what kind of wine would go well with it. This person talks about grapes and "body," information that you memorize and repeat later on when you open the bottle at the table. You inhale the wine's scent, taste it, taste it again while eating, and then the comments begin. This whole process is repeated during the appetizers, entrées, desserts, and maybe also with coffee and so on even later—well, you know what I mean. Now imagine that someone at the dinner party doesn't drink alcohol and so will be left out during the smelling and tasting, and, of course, won't be able to add his or her opinions. Talk about feeling excluded. I myself have experienced how alcoholic drinks, and therefore the person imbibing alcohol, take priority over the teetotaler. With this type of lopsided treatment, guests who prefer to remain alcohol-free risk an inferior overall experience compared to those who drink alcohol. This isn't necessarily because of the non-alcoholic beverage itself; it could just as well be a result of the social setup associated with, or better yet not associated with, the beverage—the careful selection, the interest shown in its flavor, how well the beverage goes with the food, and, not least, how it is served. This often comes naturally to someone who is interested in food and drink when it comes to beverages but is mostly ignored for the alcohol-free. I hope that this book will help elevate the status of alcohol-free beverages at the table, and further assist in the inclusion of all who prefer to go alcohol-free in the social context of the dinner table.

ALCOHOLIC VERSUS NON-ALCOHOLIC

OK, let's give alcohol-free beverages their due, but it would be a lie to pretend that alcohol doesn't have a role to play. This doesn't mean that alcohol makes a drink taste better or makes it a better match to meals, but it does have certain functions that are good to be aware of (aside from its intoxicating effect, of course). The vapor from a drink containing alcohol helps transport the aromas to the nostrils, which enables us to experience the drink's subtle scents and flavors more easily. In practice, this means that we can experience—both in smell and in taste—fruitiness or other sweetness in an alcoholic wine without the wine actually being sweet. In contrast, juice will neither smell nor taste of fruit or other sweetness without actually being sweet. The subtle aromas and tastes in alcoholic beverages contribute to their flavor complexities. The tastes arrive in intervals and linger longer in the mouth. The drink becomes thrilling, more sip-friendly, and fun to analyze.

Alcohol also affects the beverage's texture and body. The higher the percentage of alcohol, the more full-bodied and creamy the beverage will taste. It is this phenomenon that makes it suitable to serve beverages with high alcohol content alongside fatty, rich, and creamy dishes. Check out aquavit at your local liquor store, for example. Apart from warming the

HEADS UP!

I use Angostura bitters in some of the recipes in this book. This is an alcoholic (44.7 percent) spice mix from Trinidad that has flavors of cacao, cardamom, bitter orange, and dried herbs. The small quantities used in the recipes bring the alcohol level in the prepared drinks to below 0.1 percent, which is still considered alcohol-free. Just leave out the Angostura if you want a totally alcohol-free drink.

body, the alcohol also generates a warm sensation in the mouth, which is important when the dishes are spicy. Heavily spiced foods feel even spicier when eaten together with a highly alcoholic beverage.

Let me also make clear that within this book's context, I don't see any reason to try to make alcohol-free beverages mimic alcoholic drinks. This is partly because it is seldom particularly successful, and partly because it doesn't showcase alcohol-free beverages in their own right. Different beverage categories have a variety of properties, and it is more fun and fruitful to work with these individual properties than to try to make the drinks something they are not. Having said that, however, there are times when you want a drink with certain properties, even when it is alcohol-free.

It isn't hard to prepare a good alcohol-free drink that goes well with a certain dish, but when the alcohol-free drink is analyzed using parameters such as taste complexity, it often comes over as a little flat and boring. Not much happens taste-wise after the first mouthful, and very few things happen in the alcohol-free drink that invite slow sipping and deep discussions about flavor. Nevertheless, it is possible to avoid the ho-hum experience by mixing the drink so that you create the sensation of layer upon layer of tastes. In the book's recipes, I often start out with a basic recipe and then proceed to add in different ingredients. Naturally, what I add depends partly on what I'm going to serve it with. Another reason for the different ingredients is to give the drink some of that complexity that I mentioned above. Different products and ingredients are allowed to add their different properties, and together make a beverage with an interesting complexity that is suitable for a special purpose or a certain prepared dish.

To return to the example of fatty and rich food that's well served by alcohol: I have sometimes replaced alcohol with an acidic element that "cuts" through the tongue's fatty layer, which otherwise would hinder the taste buds from experiencing all the flavors. This acidic element can come from several sources, such as, say, citrus fruits or vinegar, and it also contributes in creating the sensation of several layers of taste.

Maybe all this mixing of ingredients seems complicated, but it can also be seen as one of the alcohol-free beverage's big advantages. There is an innate freedom in being able to mix and match what you like, which is not always socially acceptable when it comes to beer, cider, and especially wines. If you mix a Barolo with blueberry juice or add a drop of elderberry juice to some vintage champagne, I'm afraid that the next invitation to your dinner club is more than likely to disappear somewhere along the mail route. Mixing kombucha with pineapple juice won't raise any eyebrows, nor will pouring some currant juice into a glass with cranberry juice. This freedom makes it possible for you to measure at will and balance the recipes to your personal preferences. If it is too tart, add some more sugar or agave syrup. Too sweet? Dilute it with more citrus or vinegar. Simple, isn't it? You can't really allow yourself the same freedom around beer, cider, or wine.

TASTE

A prerequisite for understanding theories around food and drink pairings is to know what we mean by taste. Our sense of taste is located in our oral cavity, i.e. the mouth, and mostly on the upper side of the tongue. It is the small receptor cells in the taste buds that react to the five different perceptions: sweet, sour, bitter, salty, and umami—i.e. the basic tastes.

How we perceive taste and what we think is tasty is highly individual. Early taste experiences, what we associate different tastes with, and what food culture we've been raised in, are all aspects of how we experience tastes. There are, however, a few simple universal rules for how the basic tastes affect each other.

Sweet. Sweetness is the taste that attracts the biggest audience. It is in mother's milk, and it is the first taste we experience as children. Sweetness is in both food and drink, and can come from pure sugar, honey, or different versions of syrup. But sweetness might also come from other ingredients which we don't associate directly with sweetness, such as oven-roasted vegetables, cream, or caramelized onions.

A good rule of thumb is to choose a beverage that equals the food's sweetness. If the drink is to be served with dessert, it is well worth contemplating serving a beverage that is sweeter than the dish because the drink may otherwise be perceived as sour. You can also choose to go a totally different way and not work with a sweet beverage at all—coffee and tea, for example, are often enjoyed with dessert or a sweet dish. There you work with bitterness and harshness to balance out the sweetness.

Sweet food makes the beverage taste: fresher, more bitter, rougher, less sweet.

A sweet beverage makes the food taste: fresher, more bitter, less salty, less sweet.

Sour. Sourness, or acidity, is another basic taste that is common in both food and drink. Achieving a good balance between the sour in food and the sour in drink is necessary for a pleasant combination experience. The beverage will taste flat and lack freshness if the food's sourness is overpowering. It is not as bad if the opposite occurs, since food is seldom as dependent on its level of sourness as a drink is.

Sourness in a beverage has a capacity to offset fatty foods and can make the whole effect seem fresher, while also making the sourness in the food less sour, or, i.e. less sharp.

Acidic food makes the beverage taste: sweeter, less fresh, less rough, less bitter.

An acidic beverage makes the food taste: sweeter, less fresh, less bitter, less hot.

Bitter. Bitterness is the least-liked flavor, and one which we often learn to appreciate later on in life. Some never learn to like it. There is nothing strange in this, as humans are instinctively cautious around bitter tastes, since bitterness can be an indication of toxicity. In food, bitterness is found in white asparagus, arugula, and endives, and even herbs like thyme and rosemary can be found bitter. Common bitter beverages are beer, grapefruit juice, and Pellegrino Sanbitter. It's best to be careful with bitterness in food, as the food's bitterness reinforces the drink's bitterness.

An example of how a slightly bitter beverage is a good fit is when fatty finger foods such as deli meats and cheeses are served. The drink's bitterness tempers the food's saltiness, and also cleanses the taste buds a little of the fats from the food.

Salt. Saltiness provides a good bridge between food and drink. The salt is usually found only in the food, where it enhances the ingredients' flavor, while softening the sweetness, sourness, and bitterness of the drink.

Umami. Umami is a Japanese word that means "delicate," or something along those lines. Umami, as a basic taste, was an unknown concept for a long time in the West. The taste existed, naturally, but it was seldom mentioned and there was no word for it in our daily vocabulary. Today, umami is an accepted basic taste even in our part of the world. Umami is found in fatty fish, shellfish, mushrooms, tomatoes, and cheese, and in many Asian food products like fish and soy sauce. It can be tricky to pair dishes containing lots of umami with beverages, but often beers with low bitterness or teas are good choices. In order to not to get lost in the tea jungle, it is a good idea to select a tea from a country where umami is an integral part of the food culture. Teas from China, Taiwan, and Japan are often good options.

SMELL

As mentioned earlier, our sense of taste can pick up five basic flavors. However, our sense of smell (olfaction) can pick up and separate more than ten thousand odorants. The olfactory cells are collected on a 0.15 square inch organ at the top of the nasal cavity. It's our olfactory sense that makes it possible for us to detect nuances in smells as well as in taste. It's commonly said that 90 percent of what we experience as taste arrives from the olfactory sense. I'm sure that many of us have lost our sense of taste at least once during the month of February. When we have a heavy cold with a stuffy nose it's only the basic tastes—the cells on the tongue—that aren't knocked out of commission. Lots of what we refer to as flavor in daily speech, such as apple or tomato flavors, are in fact smells. When we eat, our oral cavity fills with smells that move to the olfactory cells. That is what makes us erroneously believe that we're experiencing tastes. When we have a heavy cold, the ducts up to the olfactory cells are blocked and we lose our sense of taste—or should we say, smell? Smells and tastes that are perceived by the olfactory sense are also called flavors here.

Bitter food makes the beverage taste: more bitter, sweeter, rougher, hotter, less fresh.

Bitter beverage makes the food taste: more bitter, sweeter, less fresh, less salty, hotter.

Salty food makes the beverage taste: less fresh, less sweet, less rough, less bitter.

Umami in food makes the beverage taste: rougher, more bitter.

SENSORY (NERVOUS) SYSTEM

Our sensory system allows us to, among other things, feel the body (mouthfeel), texture, spiciness, effervescence, and temperature of what we put in our mouth. How we register the things we eat and drink also affects how we experience their taste. This way our sensory system can help when we combine food and drink.

Body. Body is another word for mouthfeel. A food or drink can feel light or full-bodied in the mouth. Neutral-tasting water provides a light mouthfeel, while apple must, a juice made from the crushed stems, seeds, and skin of the fruit, provides a full-bodied mouthfeel. It is possible to influence mouthfeel in different ways when food and drink are to be combined, and it often depends a bit on what the mouthfeel is based on. One way is to serve food and drink that have similar mouthfeel, in order to avoid the lighter of the two being overpowered by the other. Another option is to dampen the impression of mouthfeel in the food by combining the food with an acidic drink or a carbonated drink. The latter is often suitable if the mouthfeel is from fat in the food, as the acid and carbonation break it up and lighten the otherwise fatty impression.

Texture. Texture is just about the same as consistency, i.e. how something feels in the mouth. For example, a dish's texture can be soft, creamy, hard, crisp, crunchy, fatty, smooth, or rough. It might be worth your while to pay extra attention to fatty and smooth textures when you have to pair food and drink. Fat in food is a taste enhancer, which contributes to a food's mouthfeel. The same goes for creaminess. A creamy food, like mashed potatoes, is often perceived as full-bodied because of its consistency. The previous paragraph has a few words on how to best match a beverage to mouthfeel.

Fat can also lie like an unpleasant layer in the mouth, which makes the food feel heavy and not fresh, and which makes it a bit difficult to perceive other tastes and flavors. Therefore, it might be a good idea to break the fatty layer with something sour, carbonated, or bitter in the beverage. These work by offsetting the fat somewhat and make the whole food-drink combination more balanced and pleasurable.

Fatty food makes the drink taste: less fresh, less rough.

Spiciness. Hot spices are often a problem when combined with alcoholic beverages, as alcohol enhances the heat. Spicy foods are therefore best served with alcohol-free drinks.

Spicy hot food makes the drink taste: less sweet, less fresh, more bitter, rougher.

Carbonation. A carbonated beverage helps to clean the palate (the taste buds), which might be an advantage if the food is full-bodied and needs a beverage to offset it. The carbonated drink makes it easier and more enjoyable to cope with foods containing a lot of fat, sweetness, and saltiness.

Temperature. Temperature affects the taste sensation of both food and drink. It is worth your while to spend some time figuring out what temperature the food and drink will be at serving time. We often prefer to drink our mealtime drink cold. What we might not remember, though, is that we experience more intense taste sensations at higher temperatures. To make this even more complicated, other factors might simultaneously affect the tastes in other ways. For example, something bitter is more enjoyable at higher temperatures. A cup of tea, which is soft and pleasant to drink when warm, becomes bitter and rough when it has been standing too long and cooled down. Research also indicates that sweetness is less sensitive to temperature changes than other basic tastes.

When wine is served with food, its temperature should not be decided on willy-nilly. There are certain well-established guidelines on correct temperatures that will ensure the optimal taste balance is achieved in different types of wine. The principles behind these suggestions apply, of course, to alcohol-free beverages, too, the only difference being that they have not yet become well-established. I haven't bothered to work out anything like that either, but I have paid a little extra attention in situations where temperature is critical, or especially interesting.

There are of course other factors that affect the total taste experience. It might be the surroundings, our expectations, or how we feel. In addition, the food culture we grew up in plays a role in what we have learned to appreciate—or not—in tastes. Everything that affects our senses also affects how we experience food and drink.

HOW DO YOU COMBINE?

So how do we produce what will, hopefully, become a successful food and drink combination? I assume that you already know what dish you will be preparing, and that you're now looking for a suitable beverage to serve with it. The first step is to identify the prominent basic tastes in the food. It is the overall experience that is important, and in many cases, the accompanying dishes or the sauce served with the main ingredient will set the tone. We experience oven-roasted vegetables as sweet and yogurt-based sauces as tart. How the basic flavors of the food then affect and are affected by the different characters of drinks is explained in the previous chapter about tastes.

The next step is to identify how the dish is experienced by the sensory system. Is the dish spicy? Is it fatty? The sensory perception is usually the mouthfeel. Is it a light dish, or do the tastes fill your mouth to the brim until the adjective that comes to mind is "full-bodied"? It is often the preparation and seasoning of the dish that will be the deciding factor in how the food is perceived. This means that you can't just settle on "my dish is chicken breast, which is a low-fat meat of light character," but have to continue and think of how you will cook and season the chicken breast. You can choose from among the different ways mentioned in the former chapter on how to handle the mouthfeel of the dish.

Once you're here, you're a good part of the way toward your match. Perhaps you've already finished and have dusted yourself off. If you're not completely exhausted, keep going and try to figure out what are the most prominent ingredients in the dish. I'm not referring to the basic tastes here but those we can identify with the help of our olfactory sense. Do you smell a lot of rosemary or lemon, or is there a very obvious flavor of lamb? You can read in the next chapter all about how to work with the flavors in food and drink to reach a great combination of the two. What I want you to take away from this chapter is that you will not always find a beverage that will perfectly match everything that is on the plate. It's the overall experience that counts. Select the components that you sense most clearly with your taste buds and sensory perception, and use them, primarily, to work further.

MIRROR, COMPLEMENT, AND CONTRAST

Now we're leaving taste and sensory perception behind to focus on flavors. Flavors are subtle compared to the basic tastes, and to engage with flavors for food and drink matching is finely detailed work.

So, what you read here and now is not what is essential for success in combining food and drink. However, for those of you who wish to dig a little deeper, there are some well-established methods to refer to; you are probably familiar with them primarily in connection with wine.

To start, you'll pick a main ingredient or a prominent flavor in the dish to use as starting point in order to find a suitable beverage. The search can then begin by using one of the three following methods for flavor matching:

Mirror
Flavor mirroring means that you find the same or similar flavors in both the beverage and the food; the food and drink will smell more or less the same. Mirroring flavors is a relatively simple and sure way to achieve a successful match, since, for obvious reasons, the flavors don't collide with each other. Naturally occurring flavor mirroring happens when food and drink contain the same ingredients. For example, it might be lingonberry juice served with meatballs and lingonberry jam. A less obvious example is to serve Earl Grey tea with toast and orange marmalade. A classic combination, absolutely, but maybe you haven't thought more closely as to why this is so. The tea's bergamot oil is extracted from a citrus fruit and carries citrus-scented aromas. The citrus flavor in the tea is mirrored in the orange marmalade, so the match is a fact.

Complement

In complementing, unlike mirroring where you search for similar aromas in drinks and food, we search for aromas that complement each other. It is all about finding aromas that go well together without actually smelling the same. A few classic examples are apples with cinnamon, citrus with shellfish, and dill with fish. Aroma complementing goes on constantly in food preparation, without anyone having to call to mind a headache-inducing theory with a fancy name. When a dish is made up of carbohydrates, proteins, vegetables, and sauce, the choices are almost always from ingredients that complement each other. The same applies when the food is seasoned. A beverage could theoretically be compared to a sauce served with the food. Which sauce flavors are complementary? We willingly add rosemary to the red wine gravy, which is served with lamb, and we squeeze lemon into the melted butter to go with the fish. Flavor complementing works the same way when choosing the accompanying mealtime drink.

Contrast

Contrasting is the total opposite of the relatively simple methods of mirroring and complementing. However, if you're successful, the result can be both absolutely delicious and thrilling to boot. The problem with aroma contrasting is that it hardly deserves to be called a method. There really is no discernible logic behind successful combinations borne out of contrast. It is, first of all, difficult to provide examples of contrasting aromas, as the experience of contrasts is highly subjective. What could be a very odd and dubious combination of aromas for one person could be natural and obvious for someone else. There is also no way to tell in advance if two contrasting flavors are going to end in a successful or disastrous combination. Only experimentation will tell.

FOOD CATEGORIES

What often makes a beverage a good choice for a certain dish is the fact that it also goes well with other foods with similar characteristics. Different dishes can therefore be divided into separate categories, making it possible to talk about food and drink combinations in a more general aspect. The food categories I present below are very broad and cover a lot of different dishes, and so should be used only as a general guide. For each drink recipe, I will refer back to these food categories, but I will also provide examples of dishes I find very suited for just that recipe.

Many factors play a role when food and drink need to be matched. It's one thing to put down theories and ideas on paper, and another thing altogether to realize them on the plate and in the glass. Maybe you have had the experience of following the same recipe for a dish or a cocktail several times, but the end result is still never the same. Moreover, when the same recipe lands in other hands, the flavor is different yet again. The quality of the ingredients, the exact measurements, and timing are just a few examples of what might have an impact on the end result. Because of this, never be afraid to adjust and balance the different drink suggestions given for a certain dish to make the combination a hit for you. Also remember that it isn't always the main ingredient that is the most important in a food and drink combination. Oftentimes is it a side dish or a sauce that has the most impact on the dish's character. If, for example, you serve a pasta dish with a Gorgonzola sauce, it isn't the pasta that will be the deciding factor when you choose your beverage for the meal. Also, remember the total balance of the dish when you choose which beverage to serve and how it should be balanced.

Light and fresh food
We have, among other things, salads, whitefish, many vegetarian dishes, and poultry dishes in the light and fresh food category. Certain meat dishes, often containing pork, can also fit under the label "light." What decides if a dish is considered light and fresh is its method of preparation—minimally changing the ingredients and allowing them to keep as much of their original character as possible. Boiled, steamed, or raw food is often considered light and fresh.

Complex dishes
In this category we'll find dishes and trimmings that normally are seen as a bit tricky to match with beverages. Dishes that use distinctive spices such as cumin, curry, or cinnamon can often be seen as complex. The same applies to sharply acidic foods, like pickled foods, lingonberries, or tomatoes, and dishes with lots of umami.

Hearty and flavorful dishes
A few typical examples of what belongs in this category are: foods that have cooked over a long time together with spices, wine, and stock, which gives the dishes a concentrated and hearty flavor; a Dutch oven that has been left to simmer for hours; a piece of stew meat that mellows in a cast iron pan with a bottle of red wine; or the incredibly popular "pulled pork" dish, cooked in the oven or slow cooker.

Grilled dishes
Smoky flavors and aromas are common denominators in all grilled foods. However, the ingredients can vary between meat, fish, and poultry, as well as vegetables. It is said that the heat from the grill or fire adds to the flavor intensity in the food.

Fatty/rich foods

Traditional Swedish home-cooked dishes often contain a lot of butter, cream, cheese, and other fatty products. That's why we can easily lump these dishes in this category. But there is, of course, room here for other fatty dishes. For example: deep-fried fish and chips, a cream-based soup, risotto with plenty of cheese, or a lasagna drowning in creamy béchamel sauce.

Desserts

It's a bit difficult to defend desserts as a food category. Here we'll include all types of desserts, from the freshest fruit salad to the darkest, most full-bodied chocolate cake. Tastes, textures, and flavors spread out in all possible directions, so finding drinks that suit everything that fits under the dessert umbrella is just about impossible. However, whichever way we look at it, it is more justified to have a category for desserts than not; we're often all on the same page when it comes to what counts as dessert.

Cheese

The cheese category is at least as big as the one for dessert, and all cheeses are allowed here. A beverage—or even a group of drinks—that fits all of these hardly exists, but in the dish/drink suggestions I provide a more detailed description of what cheese goes well with a particular beverage. Keep in mind that sides such as marmalade, vegetables, crackers, and fruit, which are often served alongside cheeses, will also influence what beverage will work with what you are consuming.

BEFORE YOU START

After having worked as a bartender most of my adult life, I've got a work routine down pat. By using a structured regimen, kitchen work becomes both easier and more fun. Below are tips for things that are good to have in mind before you start on this book's recipes.

INGREDIENTS

A drink will never exceed the quality of its ingredients. This is why I want to say a few things about what you must keep in mind when you choose raw ingredients and other products for your drinks.

The quality of fruit and vegetables depends on the season, and whether they are grown locally or far abroad. It might not be a bad thing to learn when different fruits and vegetables are in season throughout the year. This way you'll know when certain ingredients can be expected to be the best quality, as well as what is sold at a reasonable price for certain occasions. If it is high season for a fruit or vegetable, there will often be plenty of options to choose from, and a lower price will reflect this.

Harvesttimes vary for different produce, so they're only on sale in the grocery stores for a short while during the year. Consequently, it might be difficult to find locally produced ingredients for the drinks. Of course, I recommend locally grown, if at all possible. The truth is that fruit and vegetables that have been transported over long distances are often harvested too early and left to ripen during the transport. Long-distance transport is also energy guzzling and bad for the environment. If the raw ingredient is locally sourced and harvested during its peak season, it means it has spent more time maturing in its natural environment and has had a chance to develop its flavors for longer. Better ingredients equal a better end product.

It's never wrong to choose organic or biodynamically grown produce, and in certain instances it is critical to do so. Pesticides collect on produce—i.e. on the peels and leaves. For example, when you use mint or basil leaves, it is important to know how they were grown. The same applies when you use fruit peel in drinks, or when flavoring simple syrups, or when making an old-fashioned shrub syrup or trimmings for a drink. You run the risk of including chemical pesticide residue and other nasty things in the drink if you use conventionally grown ingredients. The danger is minimized if the ingredient is organically grown, or, better yet, biodynamically grown.

Knowing that so many factors can affect an ingredient's quality, it is important to remember that the measurements given in the book are guidelines, not set in stone. The drink might need to be adjusted a little here and a bit there, depending on product quality and character, in order to arrive at an optimal result. Start out by tasting the ingredients you're going to use in your drink, so you know what you have to work with.

It is also important for the end result if you've juiced the fruit and vegetables yourself or if you've bought the juices ready pressed from a grocery store. There are loads of ready-made products that make it much simpler to create your drinks. Certain products are so good there really is no reason to go to the trouble of making them yourself. Apple must from certain fruit processors, kombucha, and tomato juices are some examples. It's worth remembering that ready-made products are seldom completely "pure." They often contain some form of flavor "tweaker"—like vinegar in beet juice. Certain products are also pasteurized, which can affect the taste. I recommend that you juice citrus fruits and vegetables—except tomatoes—yourself. The simplest way to juice citrus fruits is to use a manual juicer, like a Mexican Elbow juicer; vegetables are best juiced using a slow (masticating) juicer or a centrifugal juice extractor. Personally, I prefer a masticating juicer because it better handles the more difficult, less juicy ingredients such as root vegetables and leaves. Try to waste as little of the ingredients as possible; use the leftover fruit and vegetable pulp in baking or food preparation after you've juiced.

Ice is an indispensable drink ingredient. Ice can become a science in and of itself, but I will settle on a few simple tips. Don't skimp on the ice! If you make your own ice, preferably make it in 2- to 3-quart freezer bags that will produce massive ice blocks. From the big block you can chop out the clear pieces that contain few air bubbles and will therefore give off less water when melted. Plenty of ice will keep the drink fresh for longer without turning it watery.

TOOLS

I feel that creating food dishes and drinks is a handicraft, and I have built up a substantial collection of tools over the years. Equipment and glasses, that's my hobby; I feel those are things that add sophistication to the creation of a drink, and the whole food and drink experience, in addition to pulling the whole thing together.

It's completely unnecessary to buy equipment as though you were going to open your own cocktail bar in the living room just to make the drinks in this book, even if professional equipment or specially designed glasses can come in handy for some special occasions. A regular kitchen's equipment is enough. The following is a list of items that would be good to have at home in order to prepare the book's drinks. If you want to go professional, just go ahead and update and upgrade.

- » Manual citrus juicer—also called a Mexican Elbow
- » A sharp knife
- » Sets of measuring cups/spoons, and preferably a shot glass (1^1/$_3$ fl. oz.) and cocktail measuring glasses in sizes used for making the book's drinks
- » Digital kitchen scale
- » Electric kettle with temperature control
- » Tea strainer or sieve, and perhaps also a piece of cheesecloth
- » Thin, nice drink glasses
- » A muddler, or mortar and pestle
- » Bar spoon or a long-handled teaspoon
- » A masticating or a centrifugal juicer
- » A cocktail shaker—either in three or two parts. For the latter, you will also need to add a cocktail strainer. You can also use a jar with a lid, or a thermos if you don't have a shaker.
- » A French press coffee maker.

PREPARE

The drinks in the book are served cold unless the recipe indicates otherwise. Make sure that all ingredients that should be kept cold are in the refrigerator until they are to be used. I suggest that if you're making a cold drink, keep the glasses in the freezer for at least 30 minutes before the drink is to be served. That way you'll have a frosty and wonderfully chilled glass to serve the drink in. The drink should be served as soon as it is prepared. All trimmings and garnishes should be prepared in advance.

STRAIN

The drink has a more elegant feel if it doesn't contain any fruit slivers, ice cubes, or other "manufacturing" remnants, so strain the drink through a fine-mesh tea strainer or sieve before serving. Remember that carbonation doesn't hold up well to straining, so strain the drink before adding a carbonated ingredient.

MIX

There are many ways to mix a drink. The most common ones are build, stir, and shake. Your chosen method will depend on ingredients, how concentrated a drink you want, and what texture you're looking for. Build the drink if the ingredients will easily mix with each other. Building really just means to pour all ingredients directly into a glass.

A drink can also be stirred. Pour all the ingredients into a mixing glass or a pitcher with ice cubes and stir with a bar spoon or long-handled teaspoon until everything is as mixed, diluted, and cold as you want it. The advantage of stirring a drink is that you have control over important things such as temperature and concentration. You can taste test several times during the process, adjust, and serve when the drink is chilled just right, and diluted enough.

Drinks containing juices, egg, and dairy products are often shaken. You can shake the ingredients for most of the drinks if you have a cocktail shaker, a lidded container, or a thermos. Oftentimes the drinks come out better when the ingredients are shaken. The drink is well mixed and will have a softer texture from all the air incorporated by the shaking. Here are the three important things you want to achieve if you shake with ice:

» A mixed drink

» A cold drink

» A diluted drink

HEADS UP!

It's important to keep in mind not to shake hot or carbonated drinks. Drinks are topped up with carbonated liquids just before serving and are mixed carefully in order to save as much of the carbonation as possible.

BALANCE

It is important to get a balanced final result when you compose a drink, so always taste as you work. The flavors head in all directions if you've balanced it wrong, and the drink will end up a mess, too concentrated, or flat. I feel it is, first of all, these three things that decide whether a drink is balanced or not:

Sour-sweet
The right amount of acidity versus sweetness in a drink is important in how balanced the overall impression will be. How we experience acidity and sweetness, and the amount of each basic flavor that is deemed enough, however, is up to each individual. If you think the drink is too sour, you can always add some more of the original sweetener or add a sugar like honey, agave syrup, or a simple syrup. If you think the drink is too sweet, add in some more acidity, perhaps in the form of apple cider vinegar, kombucha, shrub, or citrus.

Flavor balance
The flavor type, and how much of it the ingredients contain depends on many factors. Maybe the raw ingredient was bought out of season; perhaps it was harvested too early; or it might be overripe. You need to remember this when you read drink recipes. The measurements in the book should be used as guidelines for what might lead to a balanced end product, but they might have to be adjusted depending on the ingredients' properties. As fresh fruit

and vegetables have natural flavor variations, it is doubly important to check the balance between ingredients while you're mixing the drink.

Flavor concentration
There comes a point when you've mixed water into a glass with concentrated fruit juice and you think you have added just the right amount. The mixture is not too strong and not too diluted. It is balanced. When making a drink, you can dilute the concentrate with some water, stir the drink in a mixing glass, or shake it in a cocktail shaker with ice. You can also choose to add more of any of the lighter ingredients, such as tea or soda water.

If the drink is to be shaken, taste the drink beforehand. A drink that will be topped off with soda water or something similar is taste-tested before this step, so you can adjust ingredients to achieve a balanced end result. Perhaps the pineapple is so sweet and intensely flavored that the coconut taste totally disappears. In this case you shouldn't hesitate—just ignore the recipe amounts and mix in some more coconut.

SERVE

You eat and drink with all your senses. That means that some of the experience arrives in the presentation of the drink. It is important that all items are ready in advance so that you can give a prime presentation and can serve the drink as soon as it is ready. Use a large but appropriately sized glass so the drink fills it generously. If the glass is too small, the service looks stingy and not properly thought out. By all means, use thin drinking glasses, as they make the drink experience feel posher. Don't be stingy with ice either, if the drink is supposed to be served on ice. Plenty of ice cubes keep the drink cold longer without getting it watery too quickly.

DARE TO EXPERIMENT

The book's recipes are meant as inspiration. Dare to experiment! Replace ingredients, try different measures, serve the drink at room temperature instead of chilled, etc. The current evolution of alcohol-free drinks is happening at such a speed that there will be many new interesting drinks and ingredients to play with. Just try it!

WATER

It's not recommended to work with an ice pick facing toward the palm of the hand.

Water is the most common drink in the world. Its simplicity makes it suitable with most food dishes. That's why it feels natural to go through a few short basic principles about water's behavior together with food, as a starting point for this book.

No tastes collide with water. However, if someone wants to dig a bit deeper into this subject, they can ponder what type of mouthfeel water provides, and then from there, go on to match it with food. What I'm talking about here are the small, tiny differences in water's characteristics. They are certainly not game changing, but they still have a certain influence on how water is experienced when served with food.

Carbonation and temperature are the components that influence the water's character and that is the easiest for you to affect yourself. A water with light mouthfeel is nicest served together with a light meal, like a fresh salad. On the other hand, if you're serving a hearty, flavorful dish, go with a water that has more mouthfeel. A sparkling water with a lot of carbonation provides a robust mouthfeel that balances out rich and spicy food, while a still or slightly effervescent water has a lighter mouthfeel. If you own a SodaStream machine, keep this in mind when you're preparing the mealtime water: push that button a little longer and you get more intensely sparkling water with more bubbles. If you buy your sparkling water at the grocery store, try the various brands on offer. A simple way to appreciate the difference in carbonation levels between brands is to compare the common brands San Pellegrino and Perrier, where San Pellegrino is more carbonated. Temperature testing shows that warmer water provides a fuller mouthfeel, while colder water is experienced as a lighter one.

You can flavor the water if you want to push it taste-wise toward the food you'll be serving. I'm talking about adding light notes of something like a fruit or herb, for instance, which accompanies or enhances the flavor experience of the food.

It is possible to infuse your water with just about anything you wish. Fruit, berries, or vegetables are good. Other flavor examples are fresh or dried herbs and spices. Go easy and don't overdo it if you select a very aromatic flavoring. It doesn't take many mint leaves, say, to add flavor to your pitcher of water.

It is easy to experiment with flavored water. The easiest way to go about it, when you want to combine it with food, is to figure out what would complement the main ingredient in your dish. Citrus, for example, is great with fish and shellfish, and rosemary and mint are classic complements to lamb dishes.

If you wish to decorate the water glasses, you can of course go for freshly picked ingredients. A thin slice of lemon on the rim of the glass is plenty if you serve lemon-infused water. You can also garnish the glass with something that contrasts with the water flavor. Maybe a fresh herb or spice that goes well with the flavor, and with the food you're serving. Remember that about 90 percent of what we perceive as taste is in fact due to our sense of smell, so what you choose as a garnish will affect the taste experience. If you have trouble making the garnish stay put on the rim of the glass, you can still make the drink look nice. Just add ice to the glass, fill the glass with water, and then let the garnish rest on top of the ice.

Another way to flavor water is to prepare the Mexican drink agua fresca. This is a drink that straddles the line between flavored water and juice. The fruit-based agua fresca is prepared from water and fruit, plus sugar and citrus for balance. The fruit can, however, be replaced or combined with other ingredients such as nuts, rice, or herbs. It's difficult to provide a basic recipe for agua fresca, as the proportions should be balanced depending on the ingredients you choose for flavoring the water; however, in this chapter I'll suggest a few variations that build on the basic method.

FLAVORED WATER

Plain water can be served with most foods. But if you want to offer something more interesting than a glass of tap water with the food, flavor a pitcher of water with fruits, berries, herbs, or vegetables—the only limits are your imagination and taste. What follows are two simple basic recipes for flavored still and sparkling water. Read more about how to choose suitable flavors on pages 18 to 20.

Non-sparkling water

1. Muddle (crush with a large pestle) fruits, herbs, or vegetables in a container that holds at least 2 quarts.

2. Add the water, then close the container and shake it for 5 seconds. Leave the container in the refrigerator for at least 2 hours.

3. Strain the water into a pitcher. Serve in thin water glasses.

Carbonated, sparkling water

1. Muddle the fruits, herbs, or vegetables in a container that holds at least 2 quarts.

2. Add 1 quart of plain, sparkling water and close the container. Let it sit in the refrigerator for at least 2 hours.

3. Strain off the flavoring. Add another 1 quart of plain, sparkling water just before serving. Pour into a pitcher. Serve in thin water glasses.

THIS GOES WELL WITH:
Light and fresh foods
Complex dishes
Hearty and flavorful food
Grilled foods

NON-SPARKLING PLAIN WATER
(makes 2 quarts)
2 quarts non-sparkling, cold water
Fruits, berries, herbs, or vegetables—to taste

CARBONATED, SPARKLING PLAIN WATER (makes 2 quarts)
1 quart + 1 quart carbonated water
Fruits, berries, herbs, or vegetables—to taste

TOMATO ON THE VINE WITH BASIL

An aromatic and acidic drink with lots of umami. The acidity and flavors go well with rich Italian dishes, and the tomatoes' umami is a good match with most umami-rich foods.

1. Muddle tomatoes and fresh basil in a container that holds at least 3 cups

2. Stir in the water, tomato vine, and lime. Close the container and shake it for 5 seconds. Let the container sit in the refrigerator for at least 2 hours.

3. Strain the water into a pitcher. Serve in thin water glasses.

THIS GOES WELL WITH:
Complex dishes
Rich foods

Examples of dishes:
Fresh shellfish
Avocado on toast
Pizza

ALSO TRY:
Use this flavored water to dilute an elderberry cordial to get a deliciously aromatic mealtime drink that suits similarly flavored dishes. If you find the sweetness overpowering, balance it out by squeezing in some lime juice.

½ cup (approx. 4¼ oz.)
  flavorful tomatoes, sliced
5 fresh basil leaves
2 cups water
Tomato vine, 6"
1 slice of lime

Serves: 2

HORCHATA DE ALMENDRAS

Horchata is a milky-looking drink that is served in different areas of Central and South America. This one, made with rice and almonds, is especially common in Guatemala and Mexico, where it is drunk plain as a cooling beverage with ice, or alongside spicy and flavorful dishes like tacos, mole, and quesadillas. I'm using long-grain rice here, as it imparts a soft, nutty flavor, but feel free to try it with other kinds of rice.

1. Cut the lime peel into wide strips with a potato peeler. Mix rice, almonds, lime peel, salt, and cinnamon with 3⅓ cups of water in a container that holds at least 1½ quarts. Close the container and leave it in the refrigerator for 24 hours.
2. Remove the lime peel and pour the mix into a blender. Add the sugar and blend for about 30 seconds.
3. Strain the horchata through a fine-mesh sieve or kitchen strainer into a bottle or large container.
4. Return the rice and almond mush to the blender; add 5 cups of water and blend for 30 seconds.
5. Strain the liquid into the bottle or container holding the first batch of horchata. Take a ladle and squeeze the rice and almond mush to remove as much liquid as possible. Close the container/bottle and store the horchata in the refrigerator, where it will keep for 3–5 days.
6. Serve the horchata cold in highball glasses over ice cubes.

GOES WELL WITH:
Complex dishes
Desserts

Examples of dishes:
Tacos
Quesadillas
Tiramisu

ALSO TRY:
In a blender, or using an immersion blender, mix 11⅕ fl. oz. Horchata de Almendras with 1¼ cup (6⅓ oz.) fresh or frozen and defrosted mango into a smooth drink. Serve in two highball glasses garnished with mint leaves. This drink is reminiscent of an Indian mango lassi and goes great with spicy Indian food and grilled foods.

WILL MAKE ABOUT 2 QUARTS
Peel of 1 lime
1¼ cup long-grain white rice
Approx. 7 oz. almonds, shelled
½ tsp. salt
1 cinnamon stick
3⅓ cups + 5 cups water
4 tbsp. granulated sugar

ORANGE BLOSSOM & CUCUMBER

This is a Middle Eastern–inspired thirst-quencher that complements foods from the same area. This drink is also an excellent palate cleanser between courses.

1. Muddle the cucumber in a container that holds at least 3 cups.

2. Add water and orange blossom water. Close the container and shake it for 5 seconds. Leave the container in the refrigerator for at least 2 hours.

3. Strain the water into a pitcher. Serve the drink in two thin water glasses and garnish with cucumber slices.

GOES WELL WITH:
Complex dishes

Examples of dishes:
Meze
Kale salad with chicken and tahini dressing

6 cucumber slices + 2 more for garnish
2 cups water
½ tsp. orange blossom water

Serves: 2

AYRAN GINGER FIZZ

Ayran is a drink made with yogurt, water, and salt. I drank my first Ayran with a dish of doner kebab in Berlin. As a drink, Ayran might seem a bit strange for anyone who is not used to it, but really, the drink is perfect to pair with foods like kebab, which is both flavorful and often pretty fatty. You can drink Ayran plain, but why not try this version with ginger beer? The ginger beer adds a bit of extra bite, which makes the drink even better for pairing with flavor-rich dishes.

1. Mix yogurt, lemon juice, water, and salt in a cocktail shaker or a jar with a lid.

2. Shake hard without ice for about 20 seconds so all ingredients are thoroughly mixed. If you stop here you'll have a plain Ayran, which is tasty as is.

3. Strain the Ayran into two tall glasses. Top off with ginger beer and stir carefully. Garnish with some grated cinnamon on top.

GOES WELL WITH:
Complex dishes
Hearty and flavorful dishes

Examples of dishes:
Meze
Kebabs
Indian curry

½ cup Greek yogurt
Scant ⅔ fl. oz. lemon juice
Scant 3⅓ fl. oz. water
½ tsp. salt
6¾ fl. oz. ginger beer—optional
Garnish: 1 pinch ground
   cinnamon

Serves: 2

RASPBERRY PUNCH

If you mix raspberry shrub with some water, you'll get a drink that is reminiscent of a light and tart cordial. In all its simplicity, it's an excellent mealtime drink that still shows depth. It can be difficult to pair highly acidic food with a beverage, as the drink often feels lame and boring if it has less acidity than the food. That's where this highly acidic drink comes into its own. The tartness also works as a fresh counterweight to very rich foods.

1. Mix all the ingredients in a small pitcher or a mixing glass and stir.

2. Serve in two wineglasses.

GOES WELL WITH:
Light and fresh dishes
Rich food

Examples of dishes:
Goat cheese salad with Parma ham and vinaigrette
Fish and chips

2 fl. oz. raspberry shrub
  (see p. 168)
10 fl. oz. water, plain or sparkling
12 drops Angostura
  bitters--optional

Serves: 2

PEPPERY AGUA FRESCA WITH WATERMELON

In many Southeast Asian and Central American countries, it's quite common to order fresh Agua Fresca with Watermelon as a cooling beverage. Here is a food-friendly version with freshly ground pepper and basil.

1. Place everything except the basil leaves in a blender and blend for about 20 seconds until you have a smooth liquid.

2. Add in the basil leaves. Stir with a spoon and squeeze the basil leaves against the blender container's side.

3. Strain the liquid into a pitcher and store it in the refrigerator.

4. Stir the liquid before serving. Serve in two water glasses.

GOES WELL WITH:
Complex dishes
Grilled foods

Examples of dishes:
Meze
Cold cuts
Hamburgers

ALSO TRY:
Replace the simple syrup with concentrated lingonberry juice, and the basil leaves with mint, for a drink with a fruitier flavor profile, which complements similar-tasting foods.

¾ lb. small, seedless watermelon
3½ fl. oz. water
⅓ fl. oz. lime juice
⅓ fl. oz. simple syrup
½ tsp. freshly ground black pepper
10 basil leaves

Serves: 2

SENKANJABIN WITH ELDERBERRY

Senkanjabin is a Persian drink with refreshing acidity. I have used elderberry in this recipe, as it binds together the other ingredients in a fine way. Senkanjabin works as both a mealtime beverage and a summery drink. You can also replace the still water with sparkling water if the food is especially rich.

1. In a saucepan, boil the water and sugar over high heat for 1 minute until all sugar is dissolved.

2. Remove the saucepan from the heat. Add apple cider vinegar, mint sprigs, and salt. Stir and let cool for 30 minutes.

3. Strain the liquid into a bottle that can be closed. Store the Senkanjabin in the refrigerator, where it will keep for at least 4 weeks.

The drink

1. Distribute the ingredients in two lowball glasses filled with ice cubes and stir carefully.

2. Garnish with cucumber sticks and mint sprigs

GOES WELL WITH:
Light and fresh dishes
Complex dishes

Examples of dishes:
Greek salad
Sushi
Meze

SEKANJABIN—approx. 10 fl. oz.
Just over 2 cups water
½ cup granulated sugar
1¾ fl. oz. apple cider vinegar
6 sprigs of mint
¼ tsp. salt

DRINK
3 fl. oz. Sekanjabin
6¾ fl. oz. water, still or sparkling
⅔ fl. oz. elderberry cordial
    concentrate
1 fl. oz. lime juice
Garnish: 2 cucumber slices cut
    into small sticks, fresh mint
    leaves

Serves: 2

ORANGE & FENNEL

Orange and fennel, with its note of aniseed, make a delicious flavor combination. The aromas go very well with food seasoned with saffron, and with shellfish dishes. By all means, reuse the fennel in cooking once it has added flavor to the water.

1. Muddle the orange and fennel in a container that can hold at least 3 cups.

2. Mix the water and Angostura bitters, close the container, and shake it for 5 seconds. Leave the container in the refrigerator for at least 2 hours.

3. Strain the liquid into a pitcher. Serve in thin water glasses.

GOES WELL WITH:
Complex dishes

Examples of dishes:
Bouillabaisse (a type of French fish soup)
Paella

½ orange, sliced
½ cup (approx. 4¼ oz.) fennel, sliced fine
2 cups water
12 drops of Angostura bitters—optional

Serves: 2

WATERMELON & ROSEMARY

Watermelon and rosemary is a somewhat unexpected flavor combination but a very successful one all the same. The flavorings' aromas give the water a push, directing it toward some more flavor-intense dishes, and the watermelon's sweetness even adds a certain full mouthfeel to the water.

1. Muddle the watermelon and sprig of rosemary in a container that holds at least 3 cups.

2. Mix the water, close the container, and shake it for 5 seconds. Leave the container in the refrigerator for at least 2 hours.

3. Strain the water into a pitcher. Serve in thin water glasses.

GOES WELL WITH:
Hearty and flavor-rich dishes

Examples of dishes:
Pasta with meat sauce
Pulled pork

½ cup (approx. 4¼ oz.)
  watermelon, cubed
1 sprig rosemary
2 cups water

Serves: 2

JUNIPER BERRY COFFEE WITH TONIC

A simple and tasty version of the yuppie classic espresso and tonic. This refreshingly cold coffee drink has its place at coffee breaks with a bagel or cookie.

1. Mix coffee and juniper berry syrup in a small pitcher and stir.

2. Fill two lowball glasses with ice cubes and pour in tonic water. Top with the coffee and juniper mixture.

3. Squeeze the lemon peel oil over the drinks and throw away the peel. Garnish with sprigs of rosemary.

GOES WELL WITH:
Rich food
Desserts

Examples of dishes:
Bagel with cold-smoked salmon (lox) and cream cheese
Grilled ham-and-cheese sandwich (croque monsieur)
Carrot cake

ALSO TRY:
Replace the juniper berry syrup and plain tonic water with roasted coconut syrup (see p. 165) and elderberry tonic, and skip the rosemary. This will produce a nuttier and fruitier drink that goes well with desserts such as hazelnut cake and banana cake, or simply makes a tasty, bracing drink.

5½ fl. oz. cold-brewed coffee (see p. 167)
⅔ fl. oz. juniper berry syrup (see p. 164)
6 fl. oz. tonic water—preferably Fentimans or Fever-Tree
Garnish: 2 lemon zests, 2 sprigs of rosemary

Serves: 2

JUICE

Consciously and elegantly combining food and juice is a relatively new phenomenon. The philosophy and know-how, which started being put into practice in a few high-end restaurants about 10 years ago, have today led to easier access to a larger supply of fine food juices. You can special-order juices or make your own from all kinds of combinations, and also from less commonly used parts of the vegetable kingdom. In this book I have used what is readily available in a well-stocked grocery store or high-end wine store.

You can squeeze the juice for the recipes yourself, but you can also buy them ready-made. It is important to remember—whether you use store-bought juices or make your own—that the juice is only as good as the quality of its ingredients. An advantage of pressing your own juice is that you'll control what goes into it. For example, you can decide on the acidity of the citrus or how sweet you want the carrot juice.

To make your own juice you'll need a centrifugal juicer, or a slow—masticating—juicer. The drum in the centrifugal juicer rotates, just as the name indicates, and expresses the fruit or vegetable juices. The centrifugal drum spins quickly and suits all juicier ingredients. It's worth remembering that juice from a centrifugal juicer tends to oxidize quickly, as a lot of oxygen is added to the juice during the juicing process. This makes it difficult to store this juice for a prolonged period.

If you want juice from less juicy fruits and vegetables, you'll need a slow (masticating) juicer. The masticating juicer is slower because it expresses the juice by using pressure. Juice from a slow juicer is more fiber-rich than a centrifugally expressed juice, and therefore slightly fuller bodied. I will have juiced fresh fruits and vegetables with a slow juicer (a Witt by Kuvings C9600W) unless the text mentions otherwise. For citrus fruits I use a "Mexican Elbow" juicer (see p. 25) because it is easier and quicker. When I have used store-bought juices, I'll suggest brand names that I especially like. Several different brands worked just fine if none in particular are recommended.

It is important to remember when you work with juices that raw ingredients can vary a lot in flavor depending on season, quality, how they've been extracted, or which brand name you buy. I strain juice through a fine-meshed sieve whether I've bought or pressed the juice myself, to avoid that "breakfast juice" flavor, and to get that decadent feeling of a "pure" mealtime drink in the glass. Don't forget to use the leftover pulp in cooking or baking if you press your own juice!

There are big variations in both the basic properties and flavors in juices. The most common basic tastes are sour and sweet, but for those of you who want more, there are also bitter, salty, and umami tastes from, say, parsnip, celery, and tomato. The possibilities are almost limitless if you want to work to mirror, complement, and contrast aromas as described on pages 18 to 20. Almost all tastes that are important in the context of food and drink in fact come from the vegetable kingdom and can be added, in one way or another, to juice.

Acidity and sweetness are nearly always relevant when I choose the ingredients I want to use to make a juice, but I use aromas too. Below you will see a small section describing how I usually work with the tastes and aromas in juices.

Fruitiness connects to the basic taste of sweetness. Fruit juice will therefore add sweetness to the drink. The fruit I will choose depends on the qualities I want the drink to reflect. It's with the fruits' aromas that I mirror, complement, or contrast the aromas in the rest of the drink's ingredients, as well as in the food. Tropical fruits like pineapple have the kind of moisture I often look for. Another type of pleasing moisture that is good to use comes from apple and pear.

Citrus adds acidity to juice. Lemon, lime, grapefruit, and orange are members of the citrus category. The fruit I select still depends on what I want to achieve with the drink. Often, it's the food to be served that guides the aroma choice. Lemon is best with fresh shellfish. On the other hand, if Mexican tacos are on the menu, I'll choose lime.

Earthiness is often something I look for when I'm serving a dish that also has earthy overtones. Perhaps it is a parsnip puree or oven-roasted root vegetables. Beets, Jerusalem artichokes, and carrots are examples of vegetables that give off an earthy flavor. You don't need to add a lot of these ingredients to a drink for their flavor to come through.

Heat and spiciness can also be achieved in juice form. I often look for heat to go with Asian dishes, grilled foods, and other foods that are associated with heat, and that may be served with a spicy sauce. Most common is to use the heat from ginger and chili peppers. I usually have spiciness in juices to complement the food's flavors. Some examples are anise-flavored fennel, which goes well with saffron, and the peppery celery root, which is good both in fresh salads and with shellfish.

Berry-like is another big category that I make use of in my juices. Berries can add sweetness, but their sweetness is not as obvious as in the fruitiness category. If the berries are prepared or cooked in any way (this goes for other fruits, too) they acquire softer, rounder characteristics with less sharp acidity and a more noticeable sweetness; just think about jams and fruit cordials. That's when they are good in a drink that will accompany dessert, or to go with a really fall-like and hearty meat dish with root vegetables and perhaps a fruity jam on the side.

A GLASS OF RED

This drink is almost as simple to mix as it is to pour a glass of wine. You'll get the same wonderful color, too. This tart currant drink goes very well taste-wise with traditional Swedish cuisine, and the drink's acidity counteracts the fat in the food.

1. Mix the ingredients in a small pitcher or a mixing glass and stir.

2. Serve in two wineglasses.

GOES WELL WITH:
Hearty and flavorful dishes
Rich food

Examples of dishes:
Sautéed deer meat
Meatballs with cream gravy
Stuffed cabbage

7½ fl. oz. blackcurrant juice—
   preferably R.W. Knudsen Just
   Black Currant Juice
4 fl. oz. cranberry juice—
   preferably Lakewood Organic
   Cranberry Juice

Serves: 2

MONSIEUR CHENG

The inspiration for this drink came while I was at a high-end Thai dinner in Melbourne, Australia a few years ago, when a similar drink was served with the flavorful and aromatic food. The coconut calms the spiciness, the carbonation counteracts the richness, and the aromatic kaffir lime leaves complement the flavors. Absolutely delicious! This is my interpretation of the drink.

1. Mix all the ingredients except the soda water in a shaker filled with ice cubes, or a jar with a lid.

2. Shake hard for 8 seconds. Strain into two highball glasses filled with ice cubes.

3. Top with soda water and stir carefully. Garnish with lime wedges and kaffir lime leaves.

GOES WELL WITH:
Complex dishes
Grilled foods
Desserts

Examples of dishes:
Chicken in green curry
Thai salad with grilled shrimps
Apple tart

ALSO TRY:
Replace the soda with kombucha flavored with ginger to get a drink with slightly higher acidity, which still suits this type of dishes.

3½ fl. oz. coconut milk, unsweetened (not the cooking variety)
3⅓ fl. oz. apple must
⅔ fl. oz. lime juice
⅔ fl. oz. agave syrup
4 fl. oz. soda water
6 kaffir lime leaves
Garnish: 2 kaffir lime leaves, 2 lime wedges

Serves: 2

JUNIPER BERRY & TONIC

A tart and bittersweet adult lemonade that is excellent both as a predinner drink and with food. This one goes extra well with rich dishes. The drink's acidity and carbonation lighten the heavy feeling that you easily end up with otherwise, in both the mouth and stomach, after a rich meal.

1. Mix juniper berry simple syrup and the lemon juice in a small pitcher or a stirring glass. Pour into two wineglasses filled with ice cubes.

2. Top each glass with 4⅓ fl. oz. tonic water and stir carefully. Garnish with lemon wedges and sprigs of rosemary.

GOES WELL WITH:
Complex dishes
Rich food

Examples of dishes:
Meze
Fish and chips
Grilled ham-and-cheese sandwich (croque monsieur)

ALSO TRY:
Replace the lemon juice with 2¾ fl. oz. freshly squeezed blood orange juice and top each glass with 3¾ fl. oz. elderberry tonic for a fruitier drink for a predinner drink, or with an Italian antipasto. Garnish with blood orange slices.

1⅓ fl. oz. juniper berry syrup
(see p. 164)
1⅓ fl. oz. lemon juice
1¾ cup tonic water—preferably
Fentimans or Fever-Tree
Garnish: 2 lemon wedges,
2 sprigs of rosemary

Serves: 2

POOR MAN'S PORT WINE

Personally, I am extremely tempted by sweet dessert wines, and port wine in particular. Port is absolutely delicious with more rustic cheeses, and with desserts containing dark chocolate. This is an alcohol-free version of that delight.

1. Mix the ingredients in a small pitcher or a stirring glass and stir.

2. Pour into two port wineglasses or small wineglasses.

GOES WELL WITH:
Desserts
Cheeses

Examples of dishes:
Chocolate and hazelnut brownies
Tiramisu
Rustic cheeses (blue cheese and washed rind cheeses,
   for example)

ALSO TRY:
For a version with greater complexity and harshness reminiscent of the tannins in red wine, mix in 7½ fl. oz. of Lakewood Organic Pure Blueberry Juice and 4 fl. oz. Agua de Jamaica, and pour it into two wineglasses. This drink goes well with dishes such as jerk chicken or pizza with chorizo, and with the same kind of cheeses as mentioned above.

6¾ fl. oz. Lakewood Organic
   Pure Blueberry Juice
1⅓ fl. oz. cherry concentrate—
   preferably Torani Cherry
   Syrup

Serves: 2

SPRING GARDEN

Seedlip Garden, an alcohol-free distilled drink with green pea, hay, and herb flavors, is included in this drink. These are exciting flavors which, together with the other ingredients, create a fresh and summery drink that are just as good when mingling as when eating dinner on the patio.

1. Mix all the ingredients except the tonic water in a small pitcher or a stirring glass.

2. Pour into two wineglasses and fill up with ice cubes.

3. Top with tonic water and stir carefully. Squeeze the oil from some Ruby Red grapefruit zest over each drink and then garnish the drinks with the zest.

GOES WELL WITH:
Light and fresh dishes
Rich food

Examples of dishes:
Salad Niçoise
Sushi
Cold-smoked salmon with dill stewed potatoes

3⅓ fl. oz. Seedlip Garden[1]
1⅓ fl. oz. rhubarb juice—
    preferably Cawston Press
    Apple and Rhubarb Juice,
    if you can't find pure rhubarb
    juice
⅔ fl. oz. elderflower cordial
6¾ fl. oz. tonic water—
    preferably Fentimans
    or Fever-Tree
Garnish: 2 Ruby Red grapefruit
    zests

Serves: 2

---

1   Available on Amazon

TRADITIONAL CRANBERRY DRINK

There are two beverages I associate with traditional Swedish home cooking: milk and lingonberry cordial. This is a version of the latter—an all-purpose drink that fits most foods. It has both a fresh acidity and sparkly effervescence. It's enjoyable on its own and is also a perfect beverage to accompany a traditional Swedish meal.

1. Mix all the ingredients except the soda water in a jar with lid that holds at least 8½ fl. oz.

2. Screw the lid on and let the jar stand in the refrigerator until serving time, preferably at least 30 minutes, to let the thyme steep and add its flavor.

3. Remove the thyme sprigs and pour the drink into two wineglasses. Top with soda water and stir carefully.

GOES WELL WITH:
Rich food

Examples of dishes:
Wallenberg (a rich veal burger made with egg and cream) with potato puree and sweetened raw lingonberry jam
Potato latkes with fried pork belly and sweetened raw lingonberry jam

7½ fl. oz. cranberry juice—preferably Lakewood Organic Cranberry Juice
⅔ fl. oz. concentrated blackcurrant cordial
⅓ fl. oz. red wine vinegar
8 sprigs of fresh thyme
3⅓ fl. oz. soda water

Serves: 2

AUTUMN PUNCH

Last fall, I was asked to create a beverage for an at-home dinner.
This is the result—a sparkling drink with fruit, vegetables, and
herbs that all contribute to an impression of fall.

1. Mix all the ingredients except the soda water in a cocktail
   shaker, or a jar with a lid, filled with ice cubes.

2. Shake hard for 8 seconds and strain the liquid into two lowball
   glasses filled with ice cubes.

3. Top with soda water and stir carefully. Garnish with fresh
   thyme.

GOES WELL WITH:
Light and fresh dishes
Rich foods
Cheeses

Examples of dishes:
Caesar salad with chicken
Ham-and-cheese quiche
Hard cheeses (like Manchego and Gruyère)

4 fl. oz. apple cider
1⅓ fl. oz. fennel juice
1⅓ fl. oz. lemon juice
⅔ fl. oz. agave syrup
⅔ fl. oz. concentrated pear
   cordial
⅓ fl. oz. apple cider vinegar
3⅓ fl. oz. soda water
Garnish: fresh thyme

Serves: 2

CHILES VIRGIN MARY

Most of us have a firm idea of what constitutes the classic brunch drink the Bloody Mary, and you either love it or hate it. For those of you who can't live without it, here is an alcohol-free version. You can adjust the spiciness of the drink by varying the amount of Chiles Virgin Mary Mix. Get the very best tomato juice you can lay your hands on—it does make a difference.

1. Put two highball glasses in the freezer for at least 30 minutes.

2. Mix the Chiles Virgin Mary Mix, tomato juice, and lemon juice in a pitcher or a stirring glass and fill it with ice cubes.

3. Stir thoroughly with a long-handled spoon so the drink gets cold and diluted enough for your taste.

4. Strain the drink into the frozen highball glasses (you can of course use ice instead of frozen glasses, if you prefer). Garnish with a lemon wedge, celery stick, and freshly ground black pepper.

GOES WELL WITH:
Complex dishes
Rich dishes

Examples of dishes:
Fresh oysters with vinaigrette
Avocado on toast
Grilled ham-and-cheese sandwich (croque monsieur)

1⅓ fl. oz. **Chiles Virgin Mary Mix** (see p. 168)
10 fl. oz. tomato juice
1 fl. oz. lemon juice
Garnish: 2 lemon wedges, 2 celery sticks, freshly ground black pepper.

Serves: 2

COFFEE JUICE

This is not a recipe that you put too much trust in before you've tried it. The combination sounds completely weird, but the drink's strong flavors meet rich food in way that is otherwise difficult to achieve with alcohol-free beverages.

1. Mix all ingredients except the Crodino in a small pitcher or a mixing glass and stir.

2. Pour into two wineglasses. Top with 1¾ fl. oz. Crodino in each glass and stir carefully. Fill the glasses with ice cubes first if you want a colder and lighter drink.

GOES WELL WITH:
Hearty and flavorful dishes
Grilled foods

Examples of dishes:
Fall stew
Beef fillet with Béarnaise sauce/port wine sauce
Grilled meats

2 fl. oz. beet juice
4 fl. oz. apple must
2 fl. oz. cold-brewed coffee
   (see p. 167)
⅓ fl. oz. apple cider vinegar
3⅓ fl. oz. Crodino[2]

Serves: 2

---

2 Available on Amazon

BACKYARD HIGHBALL

A wise person once told me that all grilled things are good. I didn't discover the charm of grilling until my father-in-law soldered together a sturdy stainless-steel grill for our summerhouse. Standing at the grill has now become one of the highlights of our stays. If, like me, you don't want to run the risk of keeping the chops on the grill for too long or letting the asparagus disappear through the grates due to a sloppy hand after a beer, then a Backyard Highball is what you need.

1. Cut a lemon in half through the middle and sprinkle some brown sugar and sea salt on the cut sides. Place the lemon halves, cut-side down, on the grill or in a frying pan over high heat. Grill the halves until they have a nice caramelized look.

2. Squeeze out the juice once the lemon halves have cooled down and strain off the lemon pulp.

3. Mix all the ingredients for the drink except the soda water in a cocktail shaker, or in a lidded jar, filled with ice cubes.

4. Shake hard for 8 seconds and strain the liquid into two highball glasses filled with ice cubes. Top with soda water and stir carefully. Garnish with mint.

GOES WELL WITH:
Grilled food

Examples of dishes:
Grilled chicken
Hamburgers
Grilled vegetables with yogurt and feta cheese

ALSO TRY:
Top with dry sparkling wine instead of soda water for a fuller and more complex taste.

2 fl. oz. lemon juice from the
  grilled lemon
2 fl. oz. orange juice
1⅓ fl. oz. lavender syrup
  (see p. 165)
6 fl. oz. soda water
Garnish: 2 mint tops

Serves: 2

GRILLED LEMON
1 lemon
1 pinch sea salt—optional
1 pinch brown sugar—optional

ROOTS & JUICE

I know this sounds a bit weird but combined with the right
food this becomes a fantastic mealtime beverage. The texture,
the tartness, and the fruitiness all provide the drink with a
fine contrast for rich and creamy dishes. It can also perfectly
complement salads with oven-roasted root vegetables, or fatty
and salty foods like cheese.

1. Mix all ingredients in a cocktail shaker, or a jar with a lid, filled
    with ice cubes.

2. Shake hard for 8 seconds and strain the liquid into two
    wineglasses filled with ice cubes. Garnish with some freshly
    ground nutmeg.

GOES WELL WITH:
Complex dishes
Rich food

Examples of dishes:
Fried halloumi with oven-roasted root vegetables
Paella
Creamy pasta dishes with saffron

8 fl. oz. orange juice
2¾ fl. oz. parsnip juice
⅓ fl. oz. apple cider vinegar
Garnish: grated nutmeg

Serves: 2

APERITIVO

I love the concept of the Italian aperitivo. It is a fantastic way to socialize over some finger foods and a drink in a relaxed way before dinner. I created this drink for my wife when we were expecting our second child. She missed her Negroni at all these aperitivo moments, and this drink became a much-appreciated alcohol-free alternative.

1. Mix all the ingredients for the drink except the rosemary soda water in a small pitcher or a mixing glass and stir.

2. Pour it into two lowball glasses filled with ice cubes. Top with rosemary soda water and stir carefully. Squeeze oil from the Ruby Red grapefruit zest over the drinks, and garnish with the zest and sprigs of rosemary

GOES WELL WITH:
Rich food
Cheeses

Examples of dishes:
Finger foods such as olives, nuts, and cold cuts
Pizza
Hard cheese (like Parmesan, Manchego, and Gruyère)

ALSO TRY:
Decrease the amount of Ruby Red grapefruit juice to 2 fl. oz. and add 1⅓ fl. oz. cold-brewed coffee (see p. 167) instead. The drink goes well with the same types of foods as mentioned above and is also very good to drink on its own.

3⅓ fl. oz. **Ruby Red grapefruit juice**
⅔ fl. oz. **concentrated blackcurrant juice**
3⅓ fl. oz. **Pellegrino Sanbitter**
4 fl. oz. **rosemary soda water** (see p. 167) or plain soda water
Garnish: **2 Ruby Red grapefruit zests, 2 sprigs of rosemary**

Serves: 2

HARVEST COLLINS

I remember well the day my slow juicer arrived because it felt just like Christmas Eve. All fruit and vegetable matter in our home's well-stocked refrigerator turned from solid to liquid state. One of the drinks created during these juice sessions was the Harvest Collins.

1. Mix all the ingredients except the tonic water in a cocktail shaker, or a jar with a lid, filled with ice cubes.

2. Shake hard for 8 seconds and strain the liquid into two highball glasses with ice cubes.

3. Top with tonic and stir carefully. Garnish with apple slices.

GOES WELL WITH:
Light and fresh foods
Rich foods

Examples of dishes:
Caesar salad with chicken
Potato latkes with crème fraîche and whitefish roe

3⅓ fl. oz. apple must
2 fl. oz. lime juice
1⅓ fl. oz. celery juice
1 fl. oz. agave syrup
4 fl. oz. tonic water—preferably
  Fentimans or Fever-Tree
Garnish: 2 thin apple slices

Serves: 2

TEA

After water, tea is the most commonly drunk beverage in the world. All tea is extracted from the leaves of the tea bush, *Camellia sinensis*. Other products are often called tea in daily speech, like rooibos, which is partly made from bush bark and stems, and chamomile, which is really a flower. To be correct, true tea only comes from leaves of the tea bush. I don't make a big deal of the difference in this book, so for simplicity's sake, this chapter also includes teas made from both chamomile and hibiscus.

Tea is a great mealtime drink and there are lots of variations. The fact that it can be drunk warm, cold, or in between gives it an enormous scope as a mealtime beverage. Perhaps even more important than temperature is that tea contains tannins. We experience a harsh texture in tannins, something often associated with red wines. This harshness makes your taste buds prepare for the next bite. The heartier the food, the more the taste buds need to get ready, and so the harsher the drink needs to be.

Tea's characteristics and properties as a mealtime beverage vary depending on where the tea was grown; which drying method was used; and if the tea has been fermented, oxidized, and stored. As mentioned, tea comes in a huge variety of styles, but it is often separated into categories by color: white, green, yellow (rare), and black. In addition, there is also the partially oxidized oolong and fermented Pu-erh teas. Rooibos is usually called red tea, but that designation is misleading here. A tea's origin can give you an indication which foods are a suitable match when you want to pair the two.

White tea is the least processed of the teas. The light color of the tea leaves is partly due to the fact that it is the buds and young leaves that are picked, and partly due to the fact that the tea has very little oxidation, if any. The Fujian province in China is known for this type of tea, but several other countries, such as India, also produce white tea. This delicate tea goes primarily with light and fresh dishes like salads without dressings, and fruit salads.

Green tea is grown primarily in China and Japan, where there are over 1,000 varieties. The leaves are green because the fresh leaves are dried to prevent oxidation. This gives the green tea a slightly "leafy" characteristic, which makes it suitable for milder foods such as rice, white meat, and fruits, like melon. Green tea can be divided into three different taste profiles, which in turn suit different types of food:

» Herby green tea with mild grass and hay flavor that goes well with shellfish and light vegetable dishes.
» Smoky green tea pairs well with lightly stir-fried dishes, mild cheeses, and white meat. Chinese green teas belong to this category.
» Fruity green tea goes well with chicken and light salads, and also works well with not-too-sweet desserts. Indian green tea belongs in this group.

Oolong—or *Wulong*, when translated from Mandarin—is mostly produced in China and Taiwan. This tea is partly oxidized and has a taste profile that lies somewhere between green and black tea. It's very versatile as mealtime beverage. The lighter oolong versions, like Tie Kun Yin, suit shellfish and rice dishes, while the heavier versions, like Tai Hong Pao, go well with heartier foods like grilled and smoked dishes. They even go well with desserts like waffles and nut cookies.

Black tea is a fully—or nearly fully—oxidized tea containing plenty of tannins, and pairs well with heavier dishes. Black tea can be divided into three taste profiles that go with different kinds of food:

» Smoky black tea—for example, Lapsang Souchong from the Wuyi Mountain in Fujian, China—goes well with grilled meats and even spice-blackened dishes. Flavorful desserts, such as pastries made with dark chocolate, also match up well with this kind of tea.
» Fruity black tea, like Darjeeling Second Flush from Darjeeling in India, goes great with spicy Indian foods and sweet fruit desserts.
» Malty black teas, like Assam tea from Assam in India, suit feta and heavier dishes.

Pu-erh comes in both green (sheng = raw) and black (shu = ripe) teas. The black variety is more common, has undergone fermentation, and has an earthy characteristic. This tea type balances fatty and rich dishes well. The more delicate versions of Pu-erh are compressed into cakes or bricks that can be stored up to twenty years. During that time, they go through a slow oxidization process, just like good wines that are laid down.

You can affect the final result of your meal no matter what type of tea you work with. It's done through the amount of tea you use in relation to the amount of water, the temperature at which you brew the tea, and how long you let it steep. As for temperature, it's known that warm tea balances fatty and rich food better than cold tea.

Tea is excellent in beverages that accompany food, and the varieties that work best are oolong, green, and black teas. White tea is very mild and can easily disappear among the other flavors, while Pu-erh is very strong and might instead often overpower other flavors. But feel free to experiment. The tea's tannins allow tea drinks to cope with heavier foods that would otherwise be difficult to match with pure juices. Green, oolong, and black tea all have good levels of tannins.

HOW TO BREW TEA

Tea is a good drink to have as is with different dishes (see previous spread for tips on how to match them), and the recipes below are meant for tea that is to be drunk plain. When you prepare tea for drinks, you usually want a strong liquid, so the tea flavor isn't lost among the other ingredients. Thus, try doubling the amount of tea leaves when you brew a tea for drinks. Using more leaves is better than steeping the tea longer.

Warm-brewed tea
When you brew tea, the amount of tea leaves, the water temperature, and steeping time depend on what type of tea you're using. Loose-leaf tea is usually of higher grade than teabags.

Always use fresh, cold tap water. Don't boil it longer than absolutely necessary and never boil the water several times. If you do, the oxygen disappears, which will have a negative effect on the flavor of the tea.

1 cup cold water
1 tsp. black tea or rooibos tea
or
2 tsp. green tea, white tea, oolong, or Pu-erh
or
1 tbsp. chamomile tea
or
0.14 oz. (approx. ¾ fl. oz.) hibiscus flowers

1   Bring the water to the correct temperature. Suitable brewing temperature depends on the variety of tea. Black tea and flower tea require hot water, about 194–203° F, in order to extract all flavor from the leaves. On the other hand, green tea will taste bitter if you use water that's too hot. 167–176° F is a suitable temperature for green and white tea. Approximately 203° F is a good temperature for oolong and Pu-erh.

2   Pour the water over the leaves. If you are using Pu-erh or oolong, you should start by rinsing the tea by pouring out the first brew after 30 seconds—this is to wash the tea and get the tea leaves to open.

3   Let the tea steep. The time varies depending on the type of tea; below are some guidelines:

Green tea: 2–3 minutes
Black tea: 3–5 minutes
Pu-erh: 3–6 minutes
Oolong: 4–5 minutes
White tea: 5–7 minutes

Rooibos tea: 5–8 minutes
Flower tea: 5–8 minutes

4   Strain off the leaves. White, green, oolong, and Pu-erh can be brewed
    several times without any problem if you want to drink more than one
    cup at a time. The aromas change between each brewing, so it might be
    a fun experiment to see how the tea experience changes with the food.
    The amount you can re-brew depends on tea variety, but it is often 2 to 3
    times.

Cold-brewed tea
When you mix tea with other ingredients and wish to drink it cold, it is often
advantageous to cold-brew it—i.e. brew the tea with cold water—and let it
steep for longer, and in the refrigerator. The tea will have softer flavors, as
cold water extracts different elements than hot water does. For instance, the
caffeine level will be lower in cold-brewed tea, which also makes it less bitter.
Cold-brewed tea is also easy to flavor, so it's a good base for creating new
drinks. Of course, it's also good to drink plain, and pleasing to combine with
food.

3¼ cup cold water
4 tsp. (approx. ⅓ oz.) tea (a bit more if these are whole leaves,
    a bit less if compressed)
or
3 tbsp. chamomile tea
or
approx. ½ oz. dried hibiscus flowers

1   Mix water and tea in a clean French press or a jar with a lid.

2   Leave the tea in the refrigerator for 6–12 hours, depending on what type
    of tea you're using. White tea will be ready first, then green tea. Rolled
    oolong, black tea, flower tea, jasmine tea, and Pu-erh must steep the
    longest. Taste test occasionally and strain the tea into a clean bottle when
    you are pleased with the flavor. Store the tea in the refrigerator, where it
    will keep for at least a week.

MORNING GLORY SIGRID!

Just behind the request for "something nice," "something tart, a bit sweet, refreshing, and perhaps pink" might be the most common request in a bar. This drink meets all the demands and it provides, thanks to the tea, a slight harshness, which is often welcome in a mealtime beverage.

1. Mix the ingredients in a cocktail shaker, or lidded jar, that holds at least 2¼ cups, filled with ice cubes.

2. Shake hard for 8 seconds. Strain into two wineglasses.

GOES WELL WITH:
Complex dishes
Grilled foods

Examples of dishes:
Meze
Tandoori chicken

1¼ cup **Earl Grey tea**—
  preferably a brand with
  a distinct bergamot flavor
1⅓ fl. oz. **raspberry shrub**
  (see p. 168)
1 fl. oz. **lemon juice**
⅓ fl. oz. **agave syrup**
⅓ tsp. **orange blossom**
  water—optional

Serves: 2

APPLE MUST & CHAMOMILE

Two drinks that are both fantastic in their own right combine here to make a great mealtime beverage. It's fresh, herby, and aromatic all at the same time, and goes well with salty and herb-seasoned dishes.

1. Brew the chamomile tea according to the instructions on p. 90 but double the quantity of tea. Let the tea cool without straining out the leaves.

2. Strain the tea into a small pitcher or a mixing glass. Add apple must and stir.

3. Serve in two wineglasses.

GOES WELL WITH:
Hearty and flavorful dishes
Grilled foods

Examples of dishes:
Onion soup
Herb and garlic grilled chicken

ALSO TRY:
Replace the apple must with a sparkling apple beverage (preferably Martinelli's) to get a more full-bodied mealtime beverage that is slightly sparkling, which goes well with similar dishes.

5½ oz. strong-brewed
   chamomile tea—preferably
   Teapigs
5½ fl. oz. apple must

Serves: 2

YUAN YANG TEA—HONG KONG STYLE

There are some things I long to eat and drink again just as soon as I've boarded the plane after a visit to Hong Kong. Yuan Yang tea is one of them. It is a combination of Ceylon tea, coffee, and condensed milk that is incredibly popular in Hong Kong and in Chinatowns all over the globe. The drink comes in both warm and cold versions, but my personal preference is to drink it cold.

Warm version.
Mix all the ingredients in two coffee cups and stir.

Cold version
Pour tea and coffee into two highball glasses filled with ice cubes. Mix in condensed milk, stir, and serve.

GOES WELL WITH:
Complex dishes

Examples of dishes:
Wonton soup with egg noodles
BBQ pork with rice and pak choi

8½ fl. oz. strong-brewed Ceylon tea
6¾ fl. oz. strong-brewed coffee—preferably medium roast
1–2 tbsp. condensed milk—to taste

Serves: 2

AGUA DE JAMAICA
WITH GINGER & CINNAMON

Many of my favorite places are in Central and South America, which I have had the good fortune to visit many times. The first time I went to this part of the world was to write my chemical engineering thesis. But instead of burying my nose in books, I learned handicraft skills from the indigenous Indian population, and I learned to dance the tango. I absorbed a lot of information about rum, pisco, mescal, and tequila, but also learned about Agua de Jamaica. The latter is a flower tea that you make by soaking dried hibiscus flowers in water, and then flavoring the tea to your taste. The hibiscus itself provides a tart flavor reminiscent of cranberries and blackcurrants.

1. In a saucepan, bring water to a boil with hibiscus flowers, ginger, cinnamon, sugar, and lime zest.

2. Turn the heat down low as soon as the mixture reaches a boil. Let it stand over low heat, covered with a lid, for about 30 minutes. Do not let it come to a boil. Once the flowers lose their color, the tea is just about ready.

3. Remove the saucepan from the heat and add the lime juice.

4. Strain the mixture into a bottle with a cork top. Store in the refrigerator until the tea is to be served. It will keep for at least 5 days.

5. Serve in two wineglasses filled with ice cubes and garnish each glass with a thin slice of lime. If needed, balance the sweetness with extra lime juice.

GOES WELL WITH:
Complex dishes
Grilled foods

Examples of dishes:
Tacos
Meze
Jerk chicken

ALSO TRY:
Divide 4 fl. oz. Agua de Jamaica and 7½ fl. oz. ginger ale between two wineglasses filled with ice cubes. Garnish with slices of lime. This version goes very well with a Thai steak salad or hamburger, and even desserts like apple pie.

MAKES ABOUT ½ QUART
2 cups water
Approx. ⅓ oz. dried hibiscus flowers
1½ tsp. freshly grated ginger
1 cinnamon stick
4 tbsp. granulated sugar
⅔ fl. oz. lime juice
Zest of 1 lime
Garnish: lime slices

FANCY TEA SHAKE

This drink is really just one example of what you can create with tea, marmalade, and vinegar. Experiment with what you have at home and create your own favorite versions!

1. Mix all the ingredients in a cocktail shaker, or a jar with lid, that will hold at least 2 cups.

2. Shake hard for about 8 seconds to make the marmalade dissolve. Strain into two small water glasses. If you want a colder drink that's a little bit lighter (less concentrated), just shake it with ice cubes.

GOES WELL WITH:
Complex dishes
Grilled foods

Examples of dishes:
Mild to medium-hot Chinese dishes
Grilled duck or pork loin

ALSO TRY:
Start out with the same recipe but pour the drink into two highball glasses filled with ice cubes and top with 1¾ fl. oz. of soda water per drink, and you'll end up with a great, refreshing and light drink for a warm summer's day.

1½ cup cold-brewed oolong tea—a stronger version like Dai Hong Pao
4 tsp. apricot marmalade— preferably St. Dalfour
1 tsp. apple cider vinegar

Serves: 2

OPEN SESAME

This is a well-balanced iced tea that is delicious with heartier, more flavorful dishes such as Indian curry, well-marinated grilled meat, or chocolate desserts. It is even great as a cooling drink on a warm summer's day.

1. Mix the ingredients in a cocktail shaker, or a lidded jar, that holds at least 2 cups.

2. Shake hard without ice for 8 seconds. Strain into two highball glasses filled with ice cubes. If you want a colder drink that's a bit lighter (less concentrated), shake it with ice cubes.

GOES WELL WITH:
Hearty and flavorful dishes
Grilled foods
Desserts

Examples of dishes:
Indian curries
Grilled chicken
Chocolate cake

1¾ cup cold-brewed **English Breakfast Tea**
2 fl. oz. yellow grapefruit juice
1 fl. oz. sesame simple syrup
(see p. 166)

Serves: 2

RICE & SHINE

Gen Mai Cha is a Japanese green tea mixed with roasted raw rice. The roasted rice imparts the beverage with a slight popcorn flavor, which adds some depth to an otherwise "grassy" tea. The fig marmalade adds sweetness, and the apple cider and the lime juice bring tartness. The mixture becomes an exciting showpiece.

1. Mix all the ingredients except the apple cider in a cocktail shaker, or lidded jar, that holds at least 2 cups.

2. Shake hard without ice for 8 seconds until all the marmalade dissolves. Strain into two wineglasses filled with ice cubes.

3. Top with sparkling apple cider and garnish with apple slices.

GOES WELL WITH:
Fatty foods
Desserts

Examples of dishes:
Risotto with green asparagus and Parmesan
Buckwheat pancakes with goat cheese, pine nuts, and honey
Crêpes with fresh fruit and chocolate sauce

4¾ fl. oz. cold-brewed Gen Mai Cha tea
2 tsp. fig marmalade—preferably St. Dalfour
⅔ fl. oz. lime juice
6¾ fl. oz. sparkling apple cider—preferably Martinelli's
Garnish: 2 thin apple slices

Serves: 2

LA FLEUR DE VIE

The inspiration for this drink came to me at a delicious afternoon tea in Paris a few years ago. I was served Jasmine tea with orange and nutmeg-flavored macarons. Of course, the environment and the atmosphere played a large part in the experience, but the memory of that afternoon tea became this drink—one that is as made for an afternoon "cuppa" or for brunch.

1. Cold-brew jasmine tea with mace, the outer layer of nutmeg, following the method on p. 91.

2. Mix the ingredients in a cocktail shaker, or a jar with a lid, that holds at least 2 cups.

3. Shake hard without ice for 8 seconds. Strain into two wineglasses filled with ice cubes. Garnish with some freshly ground nutmeg on top of the drink. If you want a colder and slightly lighter (less concentrated) drink, just include ice cubes when you shake.

GOES WELL WITH:
Rich dishes
Desserts

Examples of dishes:
Grilled ham-and-cheese sandwich (croque monsieur)
Carrot cake
Macarons

7½ fl. oz. cold-brewed jasmine
   tea with mace
3⅓ fl. oz. orange juice
⅓ fl. oz. agave syrup
⅓ tsp. turmeric juice—optional
Garnish: grated nutmeg

Serves: 2

**COLD-BREWED JASMINE TEA
WITH MACE**
Approx. ⅓ oz. jasmine tea
3 cups cold water
Approx. ⅙ oz. mace

TROPICAL MATCHA MOJITO

I knew early on that I wanted to include a version of the classic rum drink the mojito among the recipes. Somehow it still ended up being the last one I wrote down for the book. It is always difficult to find worthwhile options to already perfect classics, and it took a long time before I felt that I had created something I wouldn't be tarred and feathered for. Perhaps the classic mojito is not your idea of a mealtime beverage, but this version works well with food and also as a cooling summer drink.

1. Mix matcha, lime juice, and apple must in a matcha bowl. Whisk with a matcha whisk until the liquid is lump free.

2. Add honey and stir with a spoon until the honey has dissolved.

3. Divide the mix between two highball glasses. Pat the mint lightly and add it to the glasses.

4. Fill the glasses with ice cubes. Add ⅔ fl. oz. of pineapple juice and 2¾ fl. oz. of soda water to each glass and stir carefully. Garnish with mint.

GOES WELL WITH:
Complex dishes
Grilled foods
Desserts

Examples of dishes:
Tacos
Whole grilled fish with lemon and herbs
Crêpes with tropical fruits and chocolate sauce

2 tsp matcha tea, culinary grade
⅔ fl. oz. lime juice
4 fl. oz. clear apple must
⅔ fl. oz. liquid honey
18–20 mint leaves
1½ fl. oz. pineapple shrub
   (see p. 169)
5½ fl. oz. soda water
Garnish: 2 mint tops

Serves: 2

RED TEA PUNCH

Think of fall, hearty stews, and classic Swedish home-cooked fare. Keemun tea, with its tannins and chocolate-malty notes, is a good beverage to accompany these richer and heartier dishes. By adding blackberry shrub and citrus to enhance the tea's food characteristics, the tea becomes a perfect drink to go with a fall stew or a plate of meatballs with cream sauce.

1. Mix the ingredients in a cocktail shaker, or a jar with a lid, that holds at least 3 cups and is filled with ice cubes.

2. Shake the shaker hard for 8 seconds. Strain into two wineglasses. Garnish with the blackberries.

GOES WELL WITH:
Hearty and flavorful dishes
Grilled foods

Examples of dishes:
Boeuf Bourguignon
Grilled spareribs

1¼ cup warm-brewed, then
    cooled Keemun tea
1⅓ fl. oz. blackberry shrub
    (see p. 169)
1 fl. oz. lemon juice
⅓ fl. oz. agave syrup
12 drops Angostura bitters—
    optional
Garnish: 4 fresh blackberries

Serves: 2

KOMBUCHA

Kombucha is a sweet tea that is fermented with the help of a yeasty lump. The proud name of this yeast lump is "Symbiotic Culture of Bacteria and Yeast," but in simpler, everyday language it's known as a scoby, and in plain English we just call it a "yeast mother." This yeast "mother" consumes tea sugar and creates carbonic acid. The gooey-sweet and harsh tea turns into a refreshing, spritzy drink with fruitiness and vinegary tartness. The kombucha's flavor varies depending on what type of tea was used to make it. This beverage can also be flavored further during the brewing process while the liquid is fermenting. Being able to affect the kombucha's taste combined with its high acidity makes the drink a very suitable accompaniment to many different kinds of foods. The ready-to-consume kombucha is also full of wholesome probiotics as a result of the fermentation, and this can't be a bad thing. Also, important to mention is that kombucha does contain a tiny amount of alcohol due to fermentation, but it is still categorized as non-alcoholic if the label doesn't state otherwise.

Plain kombucha that has not been flavored during the fermentation process goes well with food with high acidic content such as salads with vinaigrette, kimchi, or pickled herrings. Another way to pair kombucha with food is to use it to contrast fatty, richer, and more flavorful foods such as creamy cheeses, falafel, or grilled sausage. Top the grilled sausage with some sauerkraut and the kombucha's tartness will kick your sausage and bread roll experience up a notch.

I opt for plain or flavored kombucha when I use it in my drink recipes, depending on what taste profile I'm looking for, and then I flavor the drink with other ingredients. But you can, of course, use other kombucha flavors than what is in the drink recipes to complement, mirror, or contrast the food's aromas.

BASIC RECIPE FOR KOMBUCHA

The kombucha will develop different characteristics depending on what tea you're using. I personally prefer black tea (regular) or oolong (more elegant and fruity). It's best to go with pure teas since ethereal oils, or flavorings, can affect the scoby. Once you are comfortable with the fermentation process, try sweetening the tea with, say, honey or agave syrup instead of granulated sugar. For best results, brew 3–5 quarts at a time.

Ingredients per quart:
1 quart water
scant ¼ cup granulated sugar
1 tbsp. tea
½ cup ready-made kombucha, either from a prior batch or unpasteurized store-bought
1 scoby, bought or homemade (see p. 170)
flavorings such as honey, fruits, or spices—optional

1. Sterilize a large glass container that has an opening of at least 4" wide in diameter, through which to pour boiling water. Wash a knife, a strainer, a set of measuring cups, a ladle, and a spoon, and then rinse them with boiling water to kill any bacteria.
2. In a saucepan, bring water and sugar to a boil and cook until the sugar has dissolved.
3. Add the tea and let it all simmer for about 6 minutes. Strain off the tea and let the liquid cool to room temperature.
4. Pour the liquid into the glass container along with the ½ cup of ready-made kombucha and the scoby. Cover the opening with a coffee filter and attach the filter with a rubber band.
5. Let the glass container sit at room temperature, in a dark area, for 7 to 10 days. In a few days the yeast "mother" will start to grow a new scoby, usually on top of her, and sediment and bubbles may start forming on the bottom of the container. This is perfectly normal. You can start taste-testing the kombucha daily after 7 days, until it has reached the balance between sweetness and acidity that you want.
6. When the kombucha is to your liking, start by lifting out, with clean hands, the "mother" and the new scoby, and then separate them. Place the two on a clean plate. The yeast "mother" gets darker with age, so it is easy to see the difference between the scobies. Both scobies are good for making new kombucha but use only one of them for each batch. It's time to put the scoby out to pasture once its color is dark brown and shifts toward black.
7. Now you have to decide whether you want to bottle the ready kombucha or if you want to flavor it. If you want to bottle it, strain the ready kombucha into clean and sterilized bottles with close-fitting corks or screw tops. Preferably drink the kombucha within a month. The kombucha might get tarter with time, as it can continue to ferment in the bottle
8. You can use fresh fruit, berries, juice, and/or spices like ginger to flavor your kombucha. Feel free to try different things. Preferably use fruit that is in season to get the best flavor. The amount of fruit, juice, and spices depends on what you decide to use. A good start is to try 20 percent of finely cut-up fruit, crushed berries, or juice to 80 percent kombucha. It is difficult to give guidelines for spices, so there you'll have to try out different amounts yourself. You can enjoy your flavored kombucha immediately if it's flavored with juice; otherwise, the kombucha and flavorings need to be kept in the container, covered with a coffee filter, for 1–2 days before you can strain the kombucha and pour it into clean bottles with close-fitting tops. Leave a 1¾ fl. oz. space at the top of the bottles and store the ready kombucha in the refrigerator.

If you want sparkling kombucha, keep the bottled kombucha in a dark area at room temperature for 1 to 3 more days. That way a second fermentation will start in the bottle. Then store the bottles in the refrigerator. Be extra careful when you open the bottles, as it is difficult to judge exactly how much pressure has built up in them.

DALECARLIA WOODS

I really enjoy taking walks in the woods when I'm visiting at home in the Swedish province of Dalarna, also known as Dalecarlia. Here is an uncomplicated tart drink with flavors of rosemary, juniper berries, and apple that was created in my head during a longer fall walk. This one almost shouts fall and hearty, long-simmering foods.

1. Mix apple must, juniper simple syrup, and Angostura bitters in a small pitcher or in a mixing glass and stir.

2. Pour into two wineglasses filled with ice cubes. Top with kombucha and stir carefully. Garnish with sprigs of rosemary.

GOES WELL WITH:
Complex dishes
Hearty and flavorful dishes

Examples of dishes:
Sausage and sauerkraut
Long-simmered game flank steak

ALSO TRY:
Replace the apple must with a sparkling pear drink to get a deliciously sparkling mealtime drink with a pear aroma that suits these kinds of dishes.

3⅓ fl. oz. apple must
⅔ fl. oz. juniper berry simple syrup (see p. 164)
12 drops Angostura bitters—optional
7½ fl. oz. plain kombucha
Garnish: 2 sprigs of rosemary

Serves: 2

SWEET VIOLET

Interesting non-alcoholic alternatives that are reminiscent of red wines have popped up in the grocery stores in the last few years. One of them is Roomi from the Swedish province of Dalarna. Many of my friends who don't live and breathe food and drink find this one a bit "difficult," however. They think that it lacks a "friendly sipping quality" and I understand what they mean. That's the reason why I created the following drink (using black currant juice instead of Roomi). A lot of flavors reminiscent of Roomi remain, but what I have added is a little more spiciness, sweetness, spritz, and a further dimension of acidity. The result is a drink that goes well with the same types of foods that Roomi does, but now with the desired sipping quality.

1. Mix black currant juice and Agua de Jamaica in a small pitcher or a mixing glass and stir.

2. Pour into two wineglasses. Top with kombucha and stir carefully

GOES WELL WITH:
Hearty and flavorful dishes
Grilled foods
Rich dishes

Examples of dishes:
Lentil and bean chili
Grilled pork loin
Pizza with pepperoni

4¾ fl. oz. organic black currant juice—preferably R.W. Knudsen Just Black Currant Juice
2¾ fl. oz. Agua de Jamaica with ginger and cinnamon (see p. 98)
4 fl. oz. plain kombucha

Serves: 2

BLUEBERRY HILL

Blueberries and blackcurrants are the two berries I most look forward to picking every summer. Here I'm using the blueberry drink's acidity and tannins, the blackcurrant cordial's berry sweetness, and the Angostura bitters' spiciness to create a tasty and simultaneously exciting mealtime beverage.

1. Mix organic blueberry juice, currant cordial, and Angostura bitters in a small pitcher or a mixing glass and stir.

2. Pour into two wineglasses. Top with kombucha and stir carefully.

GOES WELL WITH:
Hearty and flavorful dishes
Grilled foods

Examples of dishes:
Lasagna
Grilled ribs

4¾ fl. oz. organic blueberry juice—preferably Lakewood Organic Pure Blueberry Juice
⅔ fl. oz. blackcurrant cordial concentrate
12 drops of Angostura bitters—optional
6 fl. oz. plain kombucha

Serves: 2

RUBY RED KOMBUCHA

Here is a tart and fresh drink that goes well with fermented foods and other dishes with marked acidity. This is also excellent as a fresh before-dinner drink.

1. Start by rubbing a Ruby Red grapefruit wedge on the rim of two highball glasses and then press the damp rims against a plate covered in sea salt. Fill the glasses with ice cubes.

2. Mix Ruby Red grapefruit juice and juniper berry simple syrup in a small pitcher or mixing glass and stir.

3. Pour the liquid into the highball glasses, top with kombucha, and stir carefully. Garnish with the cucumber slices.

GOES WELL WITH:
Complex dishes

Examples of dishes:
Oven-baked salmon with pickled vegetables
Baltic herring and potatoes

4¾ fl. oz. Ruby Red grapefruit juice
⅔ fl. oz. juniper berry simple syrup (see p. 164)
6 fl. oz. plain kombucha
Garnish: 2 cucumber slices

Serves: 2

SUNRISE

This is an upgrade of the classic juice combination of carrot and orange. The kombucha adds acidity and the turmeric makes the drink a bit more filling than the otherwise closely related breakfast juice.

1. Mix all the ingredients except the kombucha in a cocktail shaker, or a jar with a lid, filled with ice cubes.

2. Shake hard for 8 seconds and strain the liquid into two wineglasses filled with ice cubes.

3. Fill up with kombucha and stir carefully. Garnish with grated nutmeg.

GOES WELL WITH:

Rich foods

Examples of dishes:
Frittata with kale
Pasta with shrimp and saffron

ALSO TRY:

You can also try my Winter Carrot version with hearty and flavorful dishes like daal, and with rich desserts like baklava. Shake 3⅓ fl. oz. of carrot juice, 2¾ fl. oz. of orange juice, ⅔ fl. oz. of roasted coconut simple syrup (see p. 165), and 1 tsp. orange water in a cocktail shaker filled with ice cubes. Pour the drink into two wineglasses filled with ice cubes, then top each glass with 2½ fl. oz. plain kombucha and stir carefully. Garnish with thin carrot slices and grated nutmeg.

4 fl. oz. carrot juice
2¾ fl. oz. orange juice
⅓ fl. oz. turmeric juice
4 fl. oz. kombucha flavored
  with ginger
Garnish: grated nutmeg

Serves: 2

GARDEN OF LIFE

This drink is good both as a refreshing cocktail to enjoy while mingling, or as a good mealtime beverage with many layers of aromas to combine with food.

1. Mix all the ingredients except the kombucha in a cocktail shaker, or a jar with a lid, filled with ice cubes.

2. Shake hard for 8 seconds and strain the drink into two highball glasses filled with ice cubes.

3. Fill up with kombucha and stir carefully. Garnish with the dill sprigs.

GOES WELL WITH:
Complex dishes

Examples of dishes:
Boiled crayfish with crown dill
Baltic herring and potatoes
Smoked salmon with pickled fennel

2 fl. oz. fennel juice
1 fl. oz. dill simple syrup
   (see p. 166)
4 fl. oz. Ruby Red grapefruit
   juice
4¾ fl. oz. plain kombucha
Garnish: 2 sprigs of dill

Serves: 2

RHUB & HONEY

What do you get when you mix good things with more good things? Well, you get Rhub & Honey, a fresh and fruity drink with a tiny bit of heat that adds a bit of an interesting touch. This is a delicious and uncomplicated taste combination that I think most will like!

1. Mix all the ingredients except the kombucha in a small pitcher or a mixing glass. Stir until the honey has dissolved.

2. Pour the liquid into two highball glasses filled with ice cubes.

3. Top with kombucha and stir carefully. Garnish with the mint tops.

GOES WELL WITH:
Light and fresh foods

Examples of dishes:
Salad Niçoise
Steak Tartare
Sushi

ALSO TRY:
Replace the rhubarb nectar with elderberry or gooseberry cordial to get another flavor profile, but which still suits the same type of dishes.

5½ fl. oz. rhubarb nectar—preferably Cawston Press Apple and Rhubarb juice, if you can't find pure rhubarb juice
⅓ fl. oz. ginger juice
⅓ fl. oz. liquid honey
6 fl. oz. plain kombucha
Garnish: 2 mint tops

Serves: 2

SPICE & CHAMOMILE

Seedlip Spice is a distilled, non-alcoholic drink with cardamom and herb flavors. Together with the other ingredients, it makes a cocktail with many interesting flavors. It works as a sipping drink in its own right but can also be paired with food.

1. Mix all the ingredients except kombucha in a cocktail shaker, or a jar with a lid, filled with ice cubes.

2. Shake hard for 8 seconds and strain the liquid into two highball glasses filled with ice cubes.

3. Top with kombucha and stir carefully. Garnish with the Ruby Red grapefruit slices.

GOES WELL WITH:
Light and fresh food
Rich foods

Examples of dishes:
Caesar salad with chicken
Cold-smoked salmon with potatoes in dill béchamel

3⅓ fl. oz. Seedlip Spice
1 fl. oz. chamomile and citrus simple syrup (see p. 166)
2 fl. oz. Ruby Red grapefruit juice
5½ fl. oz. plain kombucha
Garnish: 2 thin slices of Ruby Red grapefruit

Serves: 2

SANGRIA PRESSO

I have a soft spot for anything Spanish and Latin American. The language, the food, the tango—and the beverages, of course, like sangria. It's is a brilliant mixture of good things which for some reason has been given an undeserved bad reputation. But, viva la sangria! Nowadays, even non-alcoholic!

1. Roast the cacao nibs quickly in a frying pan over high heat.

2. Crush the cinnamon stick coarsely with a mortar and pestle.

3. Mix all the ingredients except the kombucha in a French press. Stir, and let the mixture sit for about 60 minutes in the refrigerator.

4. Add the kombucha and push the press-strainer down carefully. Serve in two wineglasses, or thin highball glasses, filled with ice cubes, and garnish with the blackberries and orange slices.

GOES WELL WITH:
Complex dishes
Grilled foods
Cheeses

Examples of dishes:
Tapas
Grilled shellfish
Hard cheeses (for example, Gruyère or Manchego)

2 tsp. cacao nibs
1 cinnamon stick
6 fl. oz. non-alcoholic red wine—
    preferably Ariel Cabernet
    Sauvignon Non-Alcoholic
    Red Wine[3]
2¾ fl. oz. orange juice
⅔ fl. oz. blackberry shrub
    (see p. 169)
12 drops Angostura bitters—
    optional
3⅓ fl. oz. plain kombucha
Garnish: 2 fresh blackberries,
    2 orange slices

Serves: 2

---

3 Available on Amazon

SCOBY COLADA

The piña colada is, in my opinion, one of the world's best drinks. Here I've created a food-friendly version that everybody should try.

1. Mix all the ingredients except the kombucha in a cocktail shaker, or a jar with a lid, filled with ice cubes.

2. Shake hard for 8 seconds and strain the drink into two wineglasses filled with ice cubes.

3. Fill up with kombucha and stir carefully. Garnish with fresh cilantro.

GOES WELL WITH:
Complex dishes
Grilled foods

Examples of dishes:
Tacos
Thai salad with shrimp
Grilled fish or shellfish

2 fl. oz. coconut water
2¾ fl. oz. pineapple juice
⅔ fl. oz. roasted coconut simple syrup (see p. 165) or agave syrup
6 fl. oz. kombucha flavored with ginger
Garnish: fresh cilantro

Serves: 2

WINE, BEER, & CIDER

Wine

What constitutes a non-alcoholic beverage? In the United States, by order of the Alcohol and Tobacco Tax and Trade Bureau (TTB), all substances with an alcohol-by-volume (ABV) content over 0.5 percent must be regulated. However, non-alcoholic wine is made from fermented grape juice, just like a traditional wine. When an alcohol-free wine is made, the alcohol level produced far exceeds the above-stated values. To arrive at the regulation amount, the alcohol is removed after fermentation in wine destined to become alcohol-free

So why make a wine that contains alcohol if we want to abstain? Well, in this case, it's because when the undesirable alcohol is created, so are many of the smells and flavors that give wine its special wine characteristics. There is no wine without fermentation. So, in short, all alcohol-free wines start out containing alcohol.

There are three commercially viable ways to remove the alcohol. They all contain the same three stages, but they use different methods. First, all the evanescent aromas, i.e. what we experience as smells and tastes, are saved. Then the alcohol is separated from the liquid. Once we've dumped the alcohol, the precious aromas are reintroduced to the now alcohol-free liquid. Anyone seeking a more in-depth explanation will find more to read on reverse osmosis, vacuum distilling, and spinning cone technology elsewhere.

It doesn't matter which technology is employed to separate the alcohol from the wine, because it's not only the intoxicating aspect that disappears, but also some of the full-bodied impression you get from an alcoholic wine. Also, alcohol is typically a flavor-carrier. Alcohol is a flavor enhancer in wine, just like salt is in food. All this is affected when the alcohol is removed. Consequently, we have to place non-alcoholic wine in a category of its own, slightly apart from its alcohol-containing cousin, so as not to be disappointed by its performance. You just can't expect the non-alcoholic wine to taste the same, or have the same properties, as the alcoholic wine. Having said that, there are instances when even alcohol-free wine can shine and is well worth the expense.

Beer

Alcohol-free beer has been manufactured since the days of Prohibition in the United States. It's the alcoholic beverage with the longest tradition of alcohol-free production. Alcohol-free beer is made by either removing the alcohol, or by stopping fermentation when it reaches 0.5 percent by volume so that the limit for non-alcoholic beer never is exceeded.

Just like wine, some of the beer's properties are lost with the alcohol. However, beer is relatively unharmed by limited alcohol content—to decrease a beer's alcohol content from 5 percent to 0.5 percent does not have the same invasive result to the beverage as when we decrease the alcohol content in a wine from 14 percent to 0.5 percent; this is partly because beer is originally not a very alcoholically strong beverage and partly because in beer production, you can compensate for the low alcohol level by using strong flavorings. Malt, for example, which is used in fermentation, can be made up of different cereals and can be treated in different ways to impart a certain characteristic to the beer. There is also a large amount of yeast varieties to choose from which all have different effects on the beer. Lastly, the flavor can be adjusted with hops, a beer characteristic, during fermentation, but also with citrus, berries, or other flavorings.

Beer, with its many styles and flavors, is very rewarding to work with as a mealtime beverage. Thanks to the above-mentioned flavoring possibilities, there is often a suitable non-alcoholic beer to go with what's on your plate. A general guideline when choosing beer is to match the food's flavor intensity with the beer's mouthfeel. Light beers—like light lagers, for instance—suit mild dishes, while more full-bodied beers, like Indian Pale Ale, go with heartier dishes. Do try to find common flavors in the food and accompanying drink. For example, you can find roasted and nutty notes in brown ale that goes well with grilled food items, while you may find a caramel sweetness in a light lager that will match the sweetness of oven-roasted root vegetables. Don't be afraid to use beer in drinks, and that way reach a certain balance or taste profile by mixing beer with other ingredients or drinks. In this chapter, I'll show several examples of how beer can be used in drinks.

Apple or Pear Cider

The most common procedure for making non-alcoholic cider is to stop the fermentation before it exceeds the 0.5 percent per volume limit. The non-alcoholic cider is usually half-dry to sweet. This is because a lot of the fruit sugar remains in the beverage since it hasn't been allowed to ferment into alcohol. It is precisely the sweetness in non-alcoholic cider that separates it from the alcoholic cider, which can be processed to dry. You have to take into account this sweetness when you want to combine alcohol-free cider with foods. The absolute lightest foods are out and leave their seat to the more flavorful and hearty alternatives that can better tolerate the sweetness.

It's very satisfying to make drinks with apple and pear cider. That's because the flavors are compatible with almost anything you would want to put in a drink. This makes cider a good base to build upon. A tip is to try to replace the sparkling wine in the recipes with cider. That way you'll get a drink with a fuller mouthfeel than what is suggested for the dish, and a drink that goes very well with hearty foods.

BLOOMS & BUBBLES

Festive and elegant—just like the name implies. This drink is perfect when occasions arise to raise a glass, and to accompany classic, social-event finger foods.

1. Mix apple must, chamomile simple syrup, and apple cider vinegar in a small pitcher or a mixing glass and stir.

2. Pour into two champagne glasses or coupes. Top with sparkling wine and stir carefully.

GOES WELL WITH:
Complex dishes
Fatty foods

Examples of dishes:
Canapés with whitefish roe and smetana
Canapés with chopped ham dip and apple
Canapés with sautéed chanterelle mushrooms and goat cheese

2 fl. oz. apple must
1⅓ fl. oz. chamomile and citrus
   simple syrup (see p. 166)
2 tsp. apple cider vinegar
6 fl. oz. dry, sparkling white
   wine—preferably St. Regis
   Non-Alcoholic Sparkling Brut[4]

Serves: 2

---

4 Available on Amazon

SWANKY PINEAPPLE COCKTAIL

Pineapple and bubbles. As a drink on its own or with food, this drink is simple and delicious in all situations.

1. Divide the ingredients between two wineglasses filled with ice cubes and stir carefully.

GOES WELL WITH:
Complex dishes
Grilled foods

Examples of dishes:
Vietnamese spring rolls with Nuoc Cham (dipping sauce)
Grilled salmon with hollandaise sauce

2 fl. oz. pineapple shrub
  (see p. 169)
5½ fl. oz. sparkling white
  wine—preferably St. Regis
  Non-Alcoholic Sparkling Brut
4 fl. oz. soda water

Serves: 2

CHILES MICHELADA

A well-made Michelada is the perfect drink to go with Mexican food. It's even good with grilled foods on a warm summer day. You can replace the Worcestershire sauce, soy sauce, and hot sauce with 1 fl. oz. of Chiles Virgin Mary Mix (see p. 168) if you have some. It makes the drink a bit spicier and sweeter. Do buy the very best tomato juice you can get your hands on!

1. Start by pushing a lime wedge along the rims of two highball glasses, and then hold the rims against a plate covered with tajín seasoning or celery salt.

2. Mix all the ingredients except the beer in a small pitcher or mixing glass and stir.

3. Divide the mixture between the two highball glasses and fill them with ice cubes. Top with the lager and stir carefully.

GOES WELL WITH:
Complex dishes
Grilled foods
Fatty/rich foods

Examples of dishes:
Chicken quesadillas
Tacos
Hamburgers
Avocado on toast

3⅓ fl. oz. tomato juice
1⅓ fl. oz. lime juice
⅔ fl. oz. Worcestershire sauce
1 tsp. light soy sauce
1–2 tsp. hot sauce to taste—
    preferably Cholula or Tabasco
1 bottle (11¼ fl. oz.) light lager—
    Coors Non-Alcoholic, for
    example
Garnish: 1 lime wedge, tajín
    seasoning or celery salt

Serves: 2

BITTERSWEET SPRITZER

Do you have high aspirations but a tight schedule for everything that needs to be done for the dinner party? Then this aperitif is for you. Serve it with finger foods before dinner.

1. Divide the ingredients between two champagne glasses and stir carefully. Pat the basil leaves lightly between your palms and place them in the drink.

GOES WELL WITH:
Rich foods
Cheeses

Examples of dishes:
Cold cuts
Finger foods such as olives and salted almonds
Hard cheeses (for example Manchego, Parmesan, and Gruyère)

2¾ fl. oz. Pellegrino Sanbitter
6¾ fl. oz. sparkling rosé—
   Welch's Sparkling Non-
   Alcoholic Rosé, for example
12 drops Angostura bitters—
   optional
Garnish: 2 fresh basil leaves

Serves: 2

LAGERMONADE

This is an alcohol-free version of a shandy, a mix of beer and lemonade that is commonly served in British pubs. If you want to make it super-easy, just mix half sparkling lemonade and half non-alcoholic light lager. Do experiment with other types of beers and carbonated drinks such as ginger ale.

1. Mix the grapefruit juice, dill simple syrup, and soda water in a small pitcher or in a mixing glass.

2. Pour the liquid into two wineglasses. Top with lager and stir carefully.

GOES WELL WITH:
Light and fresh foods
Complex dishes

Examples of dishes:
Salad of spring vegetables and hot-smoked salmon
Boiled crawfish with crown dill
Baltic herring and potatoes

ALSO TRY:
To get a version that also pairs well with grilled foods, mix 1 fl. oz. lemon juice and ⅔ fl. oz. concentrated elderflower cordial in a small pitcher or a mixing glass. Pour the liquid into two wineglasses and top with a light lager. This one is especially delicious with grilled fish.

2 fl. oz. yellow grapefruit juice
1 fl. oz. dill simple syrup
 (see p. 166)
2 fl. oz. soda water
1 bottle (11¼ fl. oz.) light
 lager—Coors Non-Alcoholic,
 for example

Serves: 2

GINGER SUMMIT

Inspiration for this one struck on a visit to Cognac in France a few years ago. I was served a drink made with cognac, crème de cassis, lime, and ginger ale, alongside duck confit. It was a perfect combination. This drink is also excellent served as punch.

1. Mix all the ingredients except the ginger ale in a small pitcher or mixing glass.

2. Pour the liquid into two lowball glasses or wineglasses filled with ice cubes. Top with ginger ale and stir carefully. Garnish with mint tops and cucumber slices.

GOES WELL WITH:
Grilled foods
Rich foods

Examples of dishes:
Grilled pork belly with roasted vegetables
Duck confit

4 fl. oz. Riesling with Ruby Red grapefruit, juniper berry, and rosemary (see p. 170)
⅔ fl. oz. concentrated blackcurrant cordial
⅔ fl. oz. lime juice
⅓ fl. oz. ginger juice
12 drops Angostura bitters—optional
6 fl. oz. ginger ale—preferably Fever-Tree
Garnish: 2 mint tops, 2 cucumber slices

Serves: 2

BLACKBERRY SPRITZER

This is a refreshing spritzer that is very easy to vary. Replace the soda water with ginger ale; try another shrub, or other herbs like mint and basil. It is also festive to serve this type of drink in glasses filled with ice cubes containing herbs and/or fruit (see p. 171).

1. Mix all the ingredients except the soda water in a small pitcher or mixing glass and stir.

2. Pour the liquid into two wineglasses filled with ice cubes. Top with soda water and stir carefully. Garnish with sprigs of rosemary and slices of Ruby Red grapefruit.

GOES WELL WITH:
Light and fresh foods
Complex dishes

Examples of dishes:
Pasta salad with prosciutto
Sausage and sauerkraut

4¾ fl. oz. Riesling with Ruby Red grapefruit, juniper berry, and rosemary (see p. 170)
1⅓ fl. oz. blackberry shrub (see p. 169)
12 drops Angostura bitters—optional
5½ fl. oz. soda water
Garnish: 2 rosemary sprigs, 2 slices of Ruby Red grapefruit

Serves: 2

PAN-ASIA TIKI LEMONADE

Tiki drinks belong to a category of drinks that is associated with tropical flavors, warmth, and happiness. Here is an exotic and cooling drink that suits flavorful Asian food or spicy grilled foods.

1. Mix all the ingredients except the soda water and sparkling apple drink in a cocktail shaker or a jar with a lid. Don't add ice.

2. Shake hard for 8 seconds and strain the liquid into two highball glasses filled with ice cubes. Top each glass with 1½ fl. oz. soda water and 2¾ fl. oz. of sparkling apple drink and stir carefully. Garnish with sprigs of French tarragon.

GOES WELL WITH:
Complex dishes
Grilled foods

Examples of dishes:
BBQ pork with rice and pak choi
Jerk chicken

2¾ fl. oz. pineapple juice
⅓ fl. oz. ginger juice
⅔ fl. oz. lime juice
2¾ fl. oz. soda water
5½ fl. oz. sparkling apple drink—
　preferably Martinelli's
Garnish: 2 sprigs of French
　tarragon

Serves: 2

MIMOSA MARMALADE

A mimosa is probably the perfect brunch drink. Traditionally it's made from equal parts citrus juice (often orange) and champagne or a sparkling wine. This is a simple and delicious version to serve at the same sort of occasions as its role model.

1. Mix all the ingredients except the sparkling wine in a small pitcher or mixing glass. Stir until the marmalade has dissolved.

2. Strain the liquid into two champagne glasses or coupes. Top with sparkling wine and stir carefully.

GOES WELL WITH:
Grilled foods
Rich foods
Cheeses

Examples of dishes:
Salad and grilled chicken
Pizza
Hard cheeses (for example, Manchego and Gruyère)

ALSO TRY:
Do experiment with other types of marmalade. Two other kinds I like a lot are St. Dalfour pineapple and mango marmalade, and their pear marmalade. Both work with the same type of foods as mentioned above.

4 fl. oz. orange juice
4 tsp. apricot marmalade
16 drops Angostura bitters—optional
5½ fl. oz. dry sparkling white wine—preferably St. Regis Non-Alcoholic Sparkling Brut

Serves: 2

GINGER AND BEER

When you are the parent of small children, there are times when dinner needs be on the table five minutes ago. That's just about the time it takes to make this drink. It has sweetness, spiciness, and bitterness, and is both exciting to drink and simple to prepare. Go ahead and squeeze in some lime juice if you want a tarter drink.

1. Divide all the ingredients between two beer glasses and stir carefully.

GOES WELL WITH:
Hearty and flavorful dishes
Grilled foods
Desserts

Examples of dishes:
Jambalaya
Hamburgers
Carrot cake

ALSO TRY:
Replace the 2 fl. oz. ginger ale with 2 fl. oz. apple must to make a drink with more mouthfeel that suits these types of dishes. If you think the drink is a tad too sweet, counteract the sweetness by squeezing in some lime juice.

1 bottle (11¼ fl. oz.) flavorful light beer—such as O'Doul's Premium Non-Alcoholic Beer
1 bottle (approx. 8½ oz.) ginger ale—Fever-Tree, for example
12 drops Angostura bitters—optional

Serves: 2

FRUITY HOPS

This is a simple foundation recipe for a fruity beer in which you can vary both the choice of fruit and beer. Here's the basic rule: the stronger the beer, the heartier the food you should serve it with. Return to the chapter on mirroring, complementing, and contrasting of aromas to get tips on which shrub to choose.

1. Divide the raspberry shrub between two small beer glasses. Top with beer and stir carefully.

GOES WELL WITH:
Desserts
Cheeses

Examples of dishes:
Swedish pancakes (thick crêpes) with whipped cream
   and raspberry jam
Crêpes with fresh berries and chocolate sauce
Creamy cheeses (for example, Brillat-Savarin)

ALSO TRY:
Use pineapple shrub instead of raspberry for a drink that pairs well with grilled foods, such as grilled shrimp, and complex dishes like Pad Thai and Vietnamese spring rolls.

2 fl. oz. raspberry shrub
   (see p. 168)
1 bottle (11¼ fl. oz.) flavorful
   light beer—like O'Doul's
   Premium Non-Alcoholic Beer

Serves: 2

BASIC RECIPES

Below you'll find the basic recipes for different flavorings that are good to have in the refrigerator. To give them the longest shelf-life possible, it is critical to sterilize all bottles and jars that are going to be used with hot water. Rinse the bottles and fill them with boiling water just before using them. Place the lids in a bowl and pour boiling water over them. Pour out the warm water and immediately fill the container with simple syrup or shrub. Close the container immediately and store it in the refrigerator once the contents have cooled. Simple syrup will keep for about two weeks, while a shrub can keep for several months.

SIMPLE SYRUP—approx. 10 fl. oz.

It's good to have simple syrup at home and it's very simple to make. If a drink turns out a bit too astringent, a bit of simple syrup is handy to counter the tartness without adding extra flavors. You can even experiment with flavoring the syrup by adding in fruit, spices, or herbs, or by replacing the water with juice.

6¾ fl. oz. cold water
1¼ cup granulated sugar

1. In a saucepan, bring water and sugar to a boil

2. Turn off the heat as soon the liquid starts boiling. Stir until all sugar has dissolved.

3. Pour the syrup into a clean bottle. Let cool and then store the syrup in the refrigerator where it will keep for at least 2 weeks.

JUNIPER BERRY SIMPLE SYRUP—approx. 6¾ fl. oz.

An aromatic and spicy simple syrup that is good for many things, from lemonades to adding flavor to juices such as apple, pear, and citrus.

½ cup dried juniper berries
5 fl. oz. water
6¾ fl. oz. granulated sugar
4 sprigs of fresh rosemary

1. Crush the juniper berries with a mortar and pestle. In a saucepan, bring water and sugar to a boil.

2. Lower the heat as soon as the sugar/water mixture has come to a boil and add in the juniper berries and rosemary.

3. Stir over low heat for about 5 minutes. Remove the saucepan from the heat, cover with a lid, and leave it until the mixture has cooled.

4. Strain into a clean bottle, and squeeze as much syrup you can get out of the juniper berries. Close the bottle and store the syrup in the refrigerator, where it will keep at least 2 weeks.

LAVENDER SIMPLE SYRUP—approx. 10 fl. oz.

An aromatic and herby syrup that can often be found in my bar. It goes very well together with citrus and dark berries.

6¾ fl. oz. water
1¼ cup granulated sugar
4 tbsp. dried lavender
2 sprigs of rosemary
Peel from 1 lime

1. Bring water and sugar to a boil in a saucepan.

2. Turn off the heat and add in the lavender, rosemary, and lime peel. Stir, cover with a lid, and let the mixture steep for about 60 minutes.

3. Strain the lavender simple syrup into a clean bottle, close it, and keep it in the refrigerator where it will keep at least 2 weeks.

ROASTED COCONUT SIMPLE SYRUP—approx. 10 fl. oz.

This simple syrup is often in my refrigerator because it goes well with everything citrusy, as well as tropical juices and root vegetable juices. You can experiment with this syrup in many of the recipes if you like coconut.

½ cup coconut flakes, unsweetened
1 cup water
1¼ cup granulated sugar
¼ tsp. salt
1 thin slice ginger

1. Roast the coconut flakes in a dry saucepan over high heat until they are golden brown. Keep a close eye on them so they don't burn!

2. Add water, sugar, salt, and ginger and stir. Increase the heat and bring it all to a boil.

3. Remove the saucepan from the heat as soon as the syrup starts boiling. Let cool to room temperature.

4. Strain the syrup into a clean glass jar and close. Keep the jar in the refrigerator overnight.

5. Remove the cooled surface fat with a spoon and strain the syrup into a clean bottle. Close and keep in the refrigerator; the syrup will keep for at least 2 weeks.

DILL SIMPLE SYRUP—approx. 10 fl. oz.

6¾ fl. oz. cold water
1¼ cup granulated sugar
1¾ cup (scant 1½ oz.) fresh dill weed

1. Mix water and sugar in a saucepan and stir. Bring to a boil. Add the dill when the water starts to boil. Lower the heat and stir until all sugar has dissolved.

2. Remove the saucepan from the heat and cover with a lid. Leave it at room temperature for 12 hours.

3. Strain the syrup into a clean bottle, close it, and store the syrup in the refrigerator; it will keep for at least 2 weeks.

CHAMOMILE AND CITRUS SIMPLE SYRUP—approx. 1½ cup

1 cup cold water
1 cup granulated sugar
4 chamomile tea bags—preferably Teapigs
2 fl. oz. lemon juice
1⅓ fl. oz. orange juice
Peel from ½ lemon
Peel from ½ orange
1 tsp. honey

1. Mix water and sugar in a saucepan and add the tea bags. Bring it all to a boil. Add the lemon juice, orange juice, lemon peel, and honey. Reduce the heat and stir until all the sugar has dissolved.

2. Turn off the heat and cover the saucepan with a lid. Leave at room temperature for 6 hours.

3. Strain the syrup into a clean bottle—squeeze out all the liquid from the teabags—and close the bottle. Store the bottle in the refrigerator; the syrup will keep for at least 2 weeks.

SESAME SIMPLE SYRUP—approx. 10 fl. oz.

½ cup sesame seeds
6¾ fl. oz. cold water
1¼ cup granulated sugar
¼ tsp. salt

1. Toast the sesame seeds in a dry saucepan over high heat until they are golden, but not burnt. Add the water, sugar, and salt. Mix and bring to a boil over high heat.

2. Remove the saucepan from the heat as soon as the water starts to boil. Cover the pan with a lid and leave it at room temperature overnight.

3. Strain the syrup into a clean bottle. Close the bottle and keep the syrup in the refrigerator; the syrup will keep at least 2 weeks.

COLD-BREWED COFFEE—approx. 8½ fl. oz.

Let coarsely ground coffee steep in water for this drink. Let it steep for about 24 hours before you strain off the water. This liquid can be drunk as is or used to flavor other drinks. The biggest difference between cold-brewed coffee and the regular method of preparing cold coffee—in which you first boil and then cool it—is that cold-brewed coffee is less bitter and acidic. Cold-brewing coffee makes it taste a little sweeter, with a cleaner flavor. If you want to drink the cold-brewed coffee as is, either dilute the concentrate with an equal amount of water or drink it with some ice or milk. It is also nice to add some agave syrup if you like it sweeter.

1¾ cup cold water
1+ oz. freshly coarse-ground coffee—preferably medium roast

1. Mix coffee and water in a French press or in a container that can be closed. Leave the mixture in the refrigerator for about 20–24 hours.

2. Strain through the French press's filter and through cheesecloth once or twice until the liquid no longer looks muddy.

3. Pour the coffee into a bottle or a jar that can be closed and keep the coffee in the refrigerator; it will keep for at least 1 week.

ROSEMARY SODA WATER

This is a simple way to create a flavored sparkling water that adds a fine note to drinks that are topped with soda water. Feel free to experiment with different types of herbs and spices.

6 sprigs of rosemary
2 cups of cold water

1. Place the rosemary sprigs in a container together with the water. Close the container and leave it in the refrigerator for 4–6 hours. Shake the container for a few seconds after a few hours.

2. Remove the sprigs and pour the soda water into a small SodaStream bottle (2 cups). Carbonate the water extra hard by holding down the SodaStream a few seconds longer than usual. Preferably use the sparkling water immediately, as it goes flat quickly.

CHILES VIRGIN MARY MIX—approx. ½ cup

I created this recipe when I ran my own bar. I usually worked on my own, so speed and precision were extremely important. It is much easier to get all drinks to taste the same and get them quickly served if you have prepared a mix in advance.

Approx. 2 fl. oz. Worcestershire sauce
¾ fl. oz. or 1 tbsp. original Tabasco sauce
½ tsp. celery salt
½ tsp. freshly ground black pepper
⅓ fl. oz. blackcurrant cordial
⅓ fl. oz. liquid honey
⅔ fl. oz. orange juice
½ tbsp. finely grated horseradish

1. Mix all the ingredients in a container and close it.

2. Shake for 10 seconds. Let sit in the refrigerator for at least 12 hours.

3. Strain the mix into a bottle. Close the bottle and keep it in the refrigerator for up to 2 weeks.

RASPBERRY SHRUB—approx. 5 fl. oz.

Making shrub is an old method of preservation that was used as early during colonial times in the US. The same recipe can be used with other types of fruit and be combined with spices and herbs.

½ cup raspberries, fresh or frozen and defrosted
2 bay leaves, preferably fresh
½ cup apple cider vinegar
½ cup granulated sugar

1. Place the raspberries in an airtight container with a lid and mash them with a fork.

2. Add the bay leaves and pour in the vinegar. Mix properly and mash the berries some more.

3. Add the lid and leave the container in the refrigerator for 4 days. Mash and mix once a day.

4. Strain the mixture into a saucepan and bring it to a boil over high heat.

5. Remove the saucepan from the heat as soon as the contents start boiling. Add the sugar and stir until it has dissolved. Remove any froth that appears on the surface with a spoon. Pour the shrub into a clean bottle and close it immediately. Let the shrub cool and then store it in the refrigerator, where it will keep for about 4 weeks.

BLACKBERRY SHRUB—approx. 5 fl. oz.

½ cup blackberries, fresh or frozen and defrosted
1 tsp. grated fresh ginger
½ cup apple cider vinegar
2¾ fl. oz. granulated sugar
⅔ fl. oz. agave syrup

1. Mix blackberries and ginger in an airtight container with a lid and mash the berries with a fork.

2. Pour in the apple cider vinegar, mix thoroughly, and mash the berries some more.

3. Add the lid and let the container stand in the refrigerator for 4 days. Mash and mix the berries once a day.

4. Strain the mixture into a saucepan and bring it to a boil over high heat.

5. Remove the saucepan from the heat as soon as the contents boil. Add the sugar and stir until it has dissolved. Remove any froth that appears on the surface with a spoon. Pour the shrub into a clean bottle and close it immediately. Let the shrub cool and then keep it in the refrigerator, where it will keep for at least 4 weeks.

PINEAPPLE SHRUB—approx. 6¾ fl. oz.

5 fl. oz. (5¼ oz) ripe pineapple, mashed
⅓ tsp. freshly ground black pepper
3 thin slices of ginger
2 sprigs of fresh French tarragon
½ cup apple cider vinegar
¼ cup granulated sugar
⅔ fl. oz. agave syrup

1. Mix pineapple, black pepper, ginger, and tarragon in an airtight container with a lid.

2. Pour in the apple cider vinegar and muddle or use a whisk, thoroughly.

3. Screw on the lid and let the mixture sit in the refrigerator for 4–5 days. Mash and mix once a day. The mixture has rested long enough when it gives off a strong smell of ripe pineapple.

4. Strain the mixture into a saucepan and bring to a boil over high heat.

5. Remove the saucepan from the heat as soon as it begins to boil. Add the sugar and stir until the sugar has dissolved. With a spoon, remove any froth that may develop on the surface. Pour the shrub into a clean bottle and close it immediately. Let it cool and store the shrub in the refrigerator, where it will keep for at least 4 weeks.

RIESLING WITH RUBY RED GRAPEFRUIT, JUNIPER BERRIES, AND ROSEMARY

I created this flavored wine when I developed the bar concept at the Fotografiska Museet (The Museum of Photography) in Stockholm, Sweden. This was, in an uncomplicated way, a way to imbue non-alcoholic drinks with flavors reminiscent of gin.

1 bottle (3+ cup) non-alcoholic Riesling—Carl Jung Riesling Non-Alcoholic Wine[5] for example
20 dried juniper berries
5 big pieces of Ruby Red grapefruit peel
3 sprigs of rosemary

1. Pour the wine into a larger bottle or container. Save the wine bottle.

2. Crush the juniper berries with a mortar and pestle and place them in the bottle or container along with the Ruby Red grapefruit peel and rosemary sprigs. Close the bottle/container and leave it in the refrigerator for at least 12 hours.

3. Strain the mixture into the wine bottle. Store in the refrigerator, where the flavored wine will keep up to 1 week.

SCOBY

1 quart water
¼ cup granulated sugar
1 tsp. tea
1 bottle unpasteurized plain kombucha—GT's Kombucha, for example

1. Sterilize a large glass container with an opening of at least 4" (10 cm/1dm) in diameter, to pour the boiling water through. Wash a knife, strainer, a set of measuring cups, ladle, and a spoon, and then rinse them in boiling water to kill any bacteria.

2. In a saucepan, bring the water and sugar to a boil, and boil until the sugar has dissolved.

3. Add the tea and let simmer about 6 minutes. Then strain off the tea and let the liquid cool to room temperature.

4. Pour the liquid into the glass container. Add a bottle of plain kombucha.

5. Cover the glass container with a coffee filter and secure it with a rubber band. Let the mixture stand in a dark place, at room temperature—the best storage temperature is about 69.8–78.8° F—for about 3–4 weeks.

6. Your mixture should have an approximately ⅓-inch-thick scoby after 3–4 weeks. The kombucha itself has quite a concentrated flavor and isn't all that tasty, but it works very well as a starting liquid for making conventional kombucha. Leave the scoby in the liquid until you're ready to make your kombucha, if you're not making it immediately. You can use the basic recipe for kombucha (see p. 114) if you want to start a kombucha straight away.

---

5 Available on Amazon

TIPS:

» If the yeast mother turns moldy, throw it and the liquid away.

» It doesn't matter if there are small holes or small physical damage to the scoby; it'll fix itself.

» The scoby gets darker with each fermentation.

» It is normal to see brown strings coming from the scoby.

» It is normal that the scoby's color changes depending on the kind of tea being used, and that it takes on its color.

» Kombucha should smell acidic and vinegary. If it starts to smell bad, it might be going moldy, or it can be a sign of something else not right. Throw everything away and start afresh.

» The start of a new scoby will look like a white layer. It can look suspiciously like mold, but don't worry—everything is fine.

» To minimize the risk of mold, drop some vinegar on top of the liquid when you start.

FLAVORED ICE CUBES

A festive way to give water or drinks that little bit of "extra" in appearance is to use flavored ice cubes. You can freeze all kinds of herbs, edible flowers, fruits, and berries in ice cube trays. You can even use cordials and juices as flavoring in ice cubes—the possibilities are endless!

Place the fruits, berries, or herbs you want to use in an ice tray, preferably a silicon tray that makes 1½" to 2" large cubes. Pour in water and place the tray in the freezer.

INDEX

THANK-YOUS!

The journey has felt lengthy at times, from idea to book, but it has never been a lonely one. To everyone who has endured, and even supported and inspired me, I give you my heartfelt thanks!

My wife *Elin*—this book would never have seen the light of day without you. You have inspired me, provided feedback, edited, and supported me! You're the very best!

Thomas, Simon, and *Stefan.* It has been absolutely fantastic to work with you. Relaxed, fun, and professional, all at the same time.

Bonnier Fakta and *Martin,* because you have given me the opportunity to write this book and for all your support along the way.

To my favorite sommelier and good friend, *Jasmin,* who early on encouraged me to get better at seeing food and beverage combinations, and who also provided feedback on the text.

Jimmie, who is great at naming drinks, and also at brainstorming.

My mom, who inspires me with her way of looking at food and flavors.

My dad, who is the reason I ended up behind a bar counter.

Caroline, Per-Arne, and *Agnes,* for all your help with the children.

My children *Sigrid* and *Olle*—just because you're you.

All the brave firebrands within the bar and restaurant trade who push the profession forward each day. It's a pleasure to develop and grow up by and with you.

And finally, many thanks to *you,* who are reading this book. Every hour I spent over this book has been worth it—if you find a recipe you like or that inspires you to create your own.

CONVERSION CHART

METRIC AND IMPERIAL CONVERSIONS

(These conversions are rounded for convenience)

Ingredient	Cups/ Tablespoons/ Teaspoons	Ounces	Grams/ Milliliters
Fruit, dried	1 cup	4 ounces	120 grams
Fruits or veggies, chopped	1 cup	5 to 7 ounces	145 to 200 grams
Fruits or veggies, puréed	1 cup	8.5 ounces	245 grams
Honey, maple syrup, or corn syrup	1 tablespoon	0.75 ounce	20 grams
Liquids: cream, milk, water, or juice	1 cup	8 fluid ounces	240 milliliters
Salt	1 teaspoon	0.2 ounces	6 grams
Spices: cinnamon, cloves, ginger, or nutmeg (ground)	1 teaspoon	0.2 ounce	5 milliliters
Sugar, brown, firmly packed	1 cup	7 ounces	200 grams
Sugar, white	1 cup/ 1 tablespoon	7 ounces/0.5 ounce	200 grams/12.5 grams
Vanilla extract	1 teaspoon	0.2 ounce	4 grams

LIQUIDS

8 fluid ounces = 1 cup = 0.5 pint
16 fluid ounces = 2 cups = 1 pint
32 fluid ounces = 4 cups = 1 quart
128 fluid ounces = 16 cups = 1 gallon